getting on with others

getting on with others

how to teach your child essential social skills

John Cooper

FINCH PUBLISHING
SYDNEY

Getting on with others
This edition first published in 2006 in Australia and New Zealand by
Finch Publishing Pty Limited, PO Box 120, Lane Cove, NSW 1595, Australia.
ABN 49 057 285 248

09 08 07 06   8 7 6 5 4 3 2

National Library of Australia Cataloguing-in-Publication entry

Cooper, John (John Arthur), 1950- .
    Getting on with others : how to teach your child essential
    social skills.

    Includes index.
    ISBN 1 876451 69 6.

    1. Social skills in children. 2. Social skills - Study and
    teaching (Early education). 3. Behavior modification. I.
    Title.

    155.418

Illustrations by Roy Bisson
Edited by Sarah Shrubb
Editorial assistance from Rosemary Peers
Text designed and typeset in Emona by J&M Typesetting
Cover design by Steve Miller – 154 Design
Cover photograph courtesy of photolibrary.com
Printed by Southwood Press

Notes We refer to your child as 'he' and 'she' in alternate chapters in the
interest of even-handedness. The 'Authors' notes' section at the back of this
book contains useful additional information and references to quoted material
in the text. Each reference is linked to the text by its relevant page number and
an identifying line entry.

Disclaimer While every care has been taken in researching and compiling the
information in this book, it is in no way intended to replace professional medical
advice and counselling. Readers are encouraged to seek such help as they deem
necessary. The author and publisher specifically disclaim any liability arising
from the application of information in this book.

Other Finch titles can be viewed at **www.finch.com.au**

To my parents who made so many sacrifices to give us a good start in life.

Contents

Foreword

Being the parent of a young child is a joy and a privilege, but achieving competence in the role is a considerable challenge, especially because, as we now know, this developmental stage is fundamental to the future wellbeing of that child. The privilege brings heavy responsibilities. An array of material, of widely varying quality, is available purporting to guide parents in this task. Such array can be overwhelming and well-meaning parents may end up more confused and dismayed than enlightened. The credentials of the person offering the guidance are of crucial importance in deciding whose suggestions to follow.

I have been aware of the research and clinical expertise of the author of this book for some 30 years, and was curious about how his professional experience might be distilled into something accessible to a non-professional readership. Sometimes experts lose the capacity over time to bridge this gap. To my delight I found that this book reflects John's capacity to engage with and relate to parents at all levels. Basic principles and some quite profound insights are refined into clear and simple strategies, illustrated by everyday examples that any parent will find intriguing.

The research tells us that Australian women are avid readers, but men are less likely to consume books and journals unless the material has been carefully crafted. This book will attract readers of either gender and, what I think is especially important, it reflects situations and experiences that men can readily identify with – it is candidly and empathically written by a father to meet the parenting aspirations of fathers as well as mothers. Metaphors and examples tend to refer to activities such as driving or washing the car, playing soccer and so on. Mothers will be disarmed and amused by this (since many consider that they understand the male psyche quite well) and fathers will be comfortable with it too.

Without reservation, I can recommend this book for parents and professionals wishing to expand their understanding of the principles and strategies involved in 'good parenting'. It will certainly have a place in my department, for parents and for the students of various disciplines – medicine, psychology, mental health – who are taught here.

Professor Bryanne Barnett
Clinical Director
Infant, Child and Adolescent Mental Health Service
Sydney Southwest Area Health Service (Western Zone)

Introduction

This book is about relationships. It starts with the relationship between you and your child. This is the first and most important relationship your child will have. This relationship will form the basis of all others. Psychologists working with parents and children have found that if a child has a secure and trusting attachment with her parents, it will set the stage for better relationships as she goes through life. This trusting relationship gives her the confidence to relate to others. This book discusses ways of building a stronger parent–child relationship and then goes on to describe how parents can teach children social skills, skills that will help them in all their relationships. In this book I draw on being a parent (of a girl and a boy), on having read thousands of research articles and books, but most of all on 30 years of clinical practice working with children and families.

Interactions with other people are possibly the most difficult area of life. We go through good and bad times with friends, relatives, partners, children, neighbours and colleagues. Almost everything we do involves some kind of social interaction. Unless you are a hermit, you will need some people skills. Relationships with others bring us our highest highs as well as our lowest lows. At home, school, work and leisure we interact with others. There are times when pulling together brings joy and accomplishment. There are times when relationships cause us pain and distress.

Some children find social situations difficult, and they are often unhappy as a result. These children all too often grow into adults who find social situations distressing. Providing children with secure family relationships and some basic social skills can give them a start so that they are more comfortable interacting with others. This gives your children more paths to choose from.

This book will not turn every child into a social butterfly who flits from one party to another. Each child will find her own path through life, and it will be hers and hers alone. The parent will be there to support her when she needs it and to give her independence where necessary. A parent nurtures her child's strengths so that she can do her very best. One task of being a parent is to ensure that your child is as accomplished as she can be in as many areas as possible. Most parents appreciate the importance of academic skills. More and more research is showing us that three other key areas are also important in a child's development — behaviour, social skills and solving social problems.

In this book parents will learn about children's behaviour and what causes problem behaviour. As we shall learn, some children are simply born not very cooperative. This in turn places stress on the parents' relationship with their child.

How parents manage behaviour problems is vitally important. Some parents are unsure of how to manage their children. They are fearful of confronting and disciplining children.

Part 1 of this book describes very effective behaviour management programs that encourage children to cooperate. The basis of these techniques is to develop a closer relationship with your child. By developing a more positive relationship and learning to manage the conflicts that arise, you will be giving your child a good start in learning about relationships. Cooperation starts at home. Most children who are disobedient at school started off learning how to be difficult at home.

Part 2 of the book describes how parents can teach children basic social skills that are important for their children's development. These skills include teaching children to listen, share and take turns.

Part 3 of the book looks at ways of teaching children about feelings. Relaxation techniques and other ways to reduce anxiety are described. Then the important steps of problem solving are given so that parents can teach their children to handle conflict situations.

1 The three keys to your child's social well-being

Across from me sat Ben, the twelve-year-old boy who had been referred to me for counselling because of anger problems. He was sullen, looked down at the floor, and had not said anything apart from occasionally mumbling 'Dunno', which, from a therapeutic point of view, did not give me a lot to work with. His teacher had told me that Ben was capable but did not apply himself, and that he did not listen and was disruptive in class. He also said that Ben was in with the wrong peer group and had bouts of uncontrollable anger.

Me: 'You got suspended from school again.'

Ben: 'Nyem.' (I took this to be a yes.)

Me: 'Your teacher said someone called you a name and you hit him.'

Ben (talking to his shoes): 'Wasn't my fault. He shouldn't have said that to me.'

Me: 'What else could you have done?'

Ben (long silence, then an alternative came into his mind): 'Kicked him?'

Me: 'Would that have had the same result? Would you have still got into trouble?'

Ben (to shoe): 'Nyem.'

Me: 'Let's try to think of a way you could have handled it that would have worked out all right for you. What else could you have done?' (We'd been doing problem solving for 3 weeks.)

Ben: 'Dunno.'

Me: 'Think hard. What else? Use your head.'

Ben (long silence followed by what I could see as a light going on inside his head — *I had got through!*): 'I KNOW! I could have headbutted him!'

Me: 'That's not what I meant by using your head.'

Yet Ben was an intelligent child: the school had assessed him and he came out above average in intelligence. He just had not learned alternatives to aggression when faced with the inevitable social challenges of school life. Compare this with Ryan, a boy of similar academic ability.

Ryan is cooperative, smiles a lot, gets on well with others, has lots of friends and has a range of non-violent ways of dealing with social conflict. On the few occasions when he has been teased he either ignored the other boys or, if that did not work, faced up to them and told them to stop without showing he was upset. Mostly he was with a group of friends, so he was rarely picked on anyway. He was generally liked by teachers and other adults.

It does not need a psychologist to work out which child is more likely to grow up into a well-adjusted adult. Yet we are seeing more Bens in our society today. In fact we are seeing more of all types of psychological disorders. Almost one in five children today has behavioural or emotional difficulties. Just 10 years ago, childhood depression was rarely diagnosed. In recent years prescriptions to children for fluoxetine (Prozac) and sertraline (Zoloft), both antidepressants, have increased fivefold. Previously there was a similar increase in prescriptions for stimulant drugs given to children with Attention Deficit Disorder (ADD). We also know that children with significant behavioural or emotional problems are more likely to grow into adults with psychological problems if they do not get help.

There are a number of important differences between Ben and Ryan:

BEN	RYAN
Ben does not cooperate with teachers.	Ryan is cooperative.
Ben lacks social skills such as eye contact. He does not smile much, does not listen, and has not learnt conversational skills.	Ryan has good social skills and gets along well with students and teachers.
Ben has little control over his emotions. When someone annoys Ben, he hits them. Ben is not a very creative problem solver.	Ryan can control his feelings. Ryan can be assertive rather than aggressive.

The differences are in three key areas:

1   cooperative behaviour
2   social skills
3   social problem solving.

These skills are learned sequentially — one builds upon the other, starting with cooperation. Let us look more closely at each of these three skills.

Cooperative behaviour

Nicola (two and a half) would not get dressed for preschool.

Dad: 'Are you cooperating?'

Nicola (looking disdainful): 'No, I'm Nicola.'

Cooperation is a basic skill. If a child does not learn to cooperate, this will affect so much of her later development. Children who do not cooperate have trouble learning other important social and problem solving skills. Like Ben, they get stuck in the same way of responding.

Ben will not do as well as Ryan in school, even though Ben is just as intelligent. Children with difficult behaviour often do not pay attention in class, and therefore they do not fulfil their potential. Ben is likely to be rejected by most other students because of his antisocial manner. Ben will probably hang around with a group of boys who also get into trouble, as these boys are the only ones who will accept his behaviour. The boys in the group will then encourage each other to perform even more outrageous behaviour. Ben's schoolwork will then deteriorate further.

Cooperative behaviour starts at home. Many children like Ben are in frequent conflict with their parents. When he was younger, Ben became more and more defiant, and his parents in turn became more and more angry and punitive. The positive, close, fun times became fewer and further between. Ben's relationship with his parents started to break down. Ben became more sullen and moody and was ready to explode at the drop of a hat. His parents described it as walking on eggshells. Ben's behaviour at home set the stage for his behaviour with peers and teachers. This was the way he knew best; it was the only way he knew.

Many children go through the terrible twos, when they throw horrendous tantrums. Most children start to grow out of these behaviours from around the age of three on-

Cooperative behaviour is a necessary first step before other social skills can be learnt.

wards. Some children, however, like Ben, do not grow out of these problems (18 percent of children continue to have significant behavioural or emotional difficulties).

Some children are at the opposite end of the spectrum. They are not disobedient and aggressive — they are shy and anxious.

> Emily was very shy at preschool. She threw tantrums in the morning before preschool and it was a battle getting her through the gate. She clung to her mother and cried. When her mother finally managed to break free and leave, Emily followed her teacher around for most of the day. She did not interact at all with the other children. The others learned to just ignore her.

Shy and anxious children are often equally stubborn and uncooperative, but instead of being aggressive, they just dig their heels in and refuse to join in with others; they also avoid new situations. They miss out on interactions with other children so do not get the practice at sharing and resolving conflicts that other children get. They often have fewer friends, which makes them a target for teasing — bullies pick on isolated children, not kids surrounded by a group of friends. Teasing has profound effects on children — imagine going into work every day and knowing that as soon as you get there others are going to make fun of you, threaten you, take your things and laugh at you.

Cooperative behaviour is a necessary first step before other social skills can be learnt. Ben had trouble learning other social skills because he was not cooperative to start with. Emily is stubborn, and if she continues her shy and anxious behaviour she will not practise and learn other social skills. She may well become a loner and vulnerable. She could well become a victim — probably bullied by Ben!

Social skills

Ryan has developed more positive social skills than Ben. Social skills include greeting others, eye contact, listening, taking turns and complimenting others. A very basic social skill such as greeting others can change the way others react. A child who looks at the other person, smiles and says 'Hello' back is likely to be spoken to more than a child who just looks down and says nothing.

Most people know how important it is to get along with others — and how difficult that can be at times. The old adage — 'It's not what you know but who you know' — is still true. Yet recent research suggests that social skills may be even more important than many people realise. The best single predictor of how a child will later adapt as an adult is not IQ, but how the child gets along with others. There is growing evidence that children with good social skills actually do better at schoolwork than other children who have similar intelligence but poorer social skills.

There is a link between social skills and psychological problems. As emotional problems in childhood are increasing, opportunities to learn social skills are actually declining. Let us look at some of the reasons for this:

- Children today spend less time interacting with other children. Children spend more time watching television than in the classroom. They also spend more time watching videos and DVDs. Playing electronic games on computers and PlayStations is also on the rise. Many parents report that children become more irritable after playing these games. Stress builds up, adrenaline is released. The purpose of adrenaline is to spur us into physical activity. Unfortunately, apart from developing great muscles in the thumb and forefinger, these games do not provide much in the way of a physical outlet.

- News reports of a child going missing strike fear into the heart of every parent. We do not consider our neighbourhoods as safe as they used to be, and children are no longer allowed to roam around with friends. Instead of an impromptu game of footy in the local park, our children are now coached in everything, which leaves less time for informal interaction and solving their own problems. Children today spend less time with other children just hanging around and learning to get along with each other, cooperate and reach compromises.

- Families have become smaller, so even in the family children have less opportunity to practise basic skills such as sharing and resolving conflicts. Sibling interaction is a key ingredient in the development of social skills. Beneficial sibling relationships can teach sharing, cooperation and conflict resolution.

Teaching children social skills gives them a choice: they can continue their self-defeating behaviours or they can use positive social skills such as sharing or taking turns. How do we help them make the correct choice, especially if they are becoming emotional? This is where social problem solving comes in.

Social problem solving

It is our emotions that get us into most trouble. Ben let his emotions rule his decision making. If someone provoked him, he got angry and hit them. He did not think ahead to the longer term consequences of his actions. I am always amazed at the difficulty many children have with coming up with solutions other than aggression. Ben got stuck in the pattern of hitting people who upset him. This is because it had immediate results:

- It stopped the teasing.
- It acted as an outlet for Ben's anger.
- It gave Ben the satisfaction of revenge.

The long-term effects, of course, are not so good:

- Ben gets suspended (again).
- He gets a negative label from teachers and children.
- Other children avoid him (or else provoke him, because

they know they will get a reaction and get Ben into trouble).

- This sets up a vicious cycle. Ben is not accepted by others, so relies on his peer group of other disruptive children for support.

As well as being unable to control their emotions, children such as Ben also have trouble reading the emotions of others. They view the world as being hostile to them. Just looking in their direction is enough to provoke aggression.

The skills of recognising and managing emotions as well as solving social problems make up what is often referred to as emotional intelligence. Some psychologists claim that emotional intelligence is more important than IQ. We do know that children who go on to have psychological problems often have great difficulty managing emotions such as anger and anxiety.

The power of parents

Parents can help children in each of the three key areas of cooperative behaviour, social skills and social problem solving skills. It is important that cooperation is taught first. If your child is not cooperative, she will not be willing to learn the other skills. Like most skills, these are best taught early. It is more difficult to teach cooperative behaviour after the age of eight. (However, there is also truth in the saying 'Never too early, never too late.' It is just that the later you leave it, the harder it is.)

Here are a few questions to ask yourself. The answers will help tell you whether or not your child has the social skills that will help her get the best start in relationships and school:

- Does your child get upset easily and have difficulty calming down?
- Is your child anxious or fearful?
- Is your child withdrawn?
- Does your child cooperate with your instructions quickly less than 60 per cent of the time?
- Is your child defiant and difficult to manage?
- Does your child argue and answer back?
- Is your child aggressive or argumentative with others?
- Is your child reluctant to join in with other children?
- Is your child reluctant to share and take turns with other children?
- Do other children ignore or keep away from your child?
- Does your child not listen (when stories are being read, for example)?

Many of the above behaviours are a sign that children will have problems learning or getting along with others. The good news is that these skills can be taught.

First, though, it is important to have an understanding of why children turn out the way they do. Both nature (the way the child is born) and nurture (how the child is brought up) are important. This is dealt with in Chapter 2.

In a nutshell

- Two children may be born with the same intelligence, but three things are important in terms of how they use it — cooperative behaviour, social skills and social problem solving.
- Most children go through phases where they throw tantrums, are angry or are very shy. Usually from three years of age, these gradually get better.
- About one in five children continues in these behaviour patterns — either defiant and angry or shy and anxious.
- Defiant or anxious children do not go on to develop the social skills and problem solving skills necessary for psychological health in later life.
- Parents can teach their children cooperative behaviour, social skills and problem solving skills.
- A positive parent–child relationship is important in developing cooperative behaviour and teaching children about relationships.

Nature or nurture?

There is an ongoing debate over whether a child's behaviour is due to nature (the way they are when they are born) or nurture (how they are brought up). The answer is both. A child's genetic make-up *and* the family environment both have important effects.

It all starts with nature

Any parent who has more than one child will know that children differ amazingly from birth. That two children can come from the same parents and yet be so different in character is often a surprise. A child's temperament or 'nature' is generally considered something that children are born with; they inherit it from their parents. You hear things like, 'He's got a sweet nature' or 'He's got a shocking temper — he's just like his father, it's in their nature.'

Parents who have children with difficult temperaments have a challenge on their hands. Such children are more difficult to settle, sleep less, are more demanding and more impulsive.

Temperamental differences can show themselves in the first few months.

Melanie had a baby girl, Katie, who was just four months old. Katie did not settle at night until about 11.00 pm and then woke every hour through the night and was wide awake again at 5.00 am. The longest Katie would sleep in the day was about 45 minutes.

Katie was irritable during the day and would cry until she was picked up. Katie would not let anyone comfort her except her parents. Even at this age she would scream if picked up by grandmas or aunties. If Melanie stopped moving, Katie would cry until she was rocked or carried around at speed. Melanie developed tendonitis in her arm from carrying Katie around while trying to do even the minimum housework. If Melanie tried to put her down, Katie would quickly work herself up into such a state that she would vomit. When in the car, Katie cried if the car stopped at traffic lights. If she was in the pram and movement was halted for longer than three seconds, she would loudly voice her displeasure.

Melanie would look on as other babies lay quietly in the pram while their mothers had a casual coffee with friends. She would overhear snippets of conversations from other mothers as she rushed past, (careful not to slow down too much), such as 'Oh and he's sleeping right through now.'

A child's temperament can have a major impact on parenting. It is much easier to look like a calm, relaxed parent when your baby sleeps through the night or lets you do the housework as he looks on contentedly. If you have a fractious baby like Katie, you are constantly tired and stressed. It is not so easy to look calm and in control. Doctors told Melanie that she was too tense. Yes, she was too tense, but this was because of Katie's behaviour.

Children who have extremely difficult temperaments are often diagnosed with Attention Deficit Disorder (ADD). It is widely believed that ADD is, at least in part, inherited. Thom Hartmann gives an interesting theory about how ADD genes may have been passed down through the generations. Hartmann believes that long ago, when societies were based on a hunter/gatherer model, people with ADD personalities were ideally suited to be hunters.

People with ADD have three main characteristics:

- They are hyperactive, fidgety and always on the go. This would have suited the hunter who had to be constantly on the move, searching for and chasing prey.
- They have a short attention span and are easily distracted. This would have been an asset to a hunter who had to continually scan the environment for scarce food and also threats from wild animals and other tribes.
- They are impulsive and act before they think. A hunter needs to act quickly and pounce on potential prey before the opportunity is lost.

Hartmann argues that, through natural selection, these genes have been passed on to other generations. As most hunters were males, this would also explain why more boys than girls have ADD.

If Hartmann's theory is correct, difficult, impulsive children would have been highly prized in earlier societies, as hunters were held in high esteem. Mothers might have said 'Oh good, he's so difficult and impulsive.' Today, children who have inherited these 'hunter' or ADD genes have to struggle with algebra and Windows XP, which their personalities are hardly suited to.

While Hartmann's theory is difficult to prove, it is a refreshing alternative to our modern view that children with ADD have a psychological disorder and need medication.

The impact of nurture

Although temperament appears to stay with the child to some extent and shape his personality, it can be modified a great deal by the way the child is parented.

Melanie persevered and survived the first very difficult year with Katie. Melanie spent a lot of time with Katie, played with her and read her books. Melanie's husband David helped out and also spent a lot of time playing with Katie. Although Katie exhausted both her parents, they pulled together. They gave Katie a warm, loving and stable environment. Gradually Katie slept more. She started talking early. She was a bright child and later did very well at school.

Katie was lucky. The caring, predictable environment gradually altered her prickly nature (although Katie can still be emotional, especially when tired).

Just as a nurturing family environment can have a very beneficial effect on parenting, a child brought up in a stressful or neglectful environment will be affected in a negative way. There are no more powerful examples of the effect of adverse environments on children than the plight of the Romanian orphans that was brought to light in the 1990s.

The conditions in which Romanian orphans were found in the 1990s shocked the world. Staffing levels and funding were woefully inadequate. Many children were malnourished and spent 18–20 hours per day lying in their cribs. The children weighed less and were shorter than average. They also had medical problems such as anaemia, Hepatitis B and intestinal worms. Most were significantly developmentally delayed — some at the age of two had not learned how to sit up — and had little speech. They also had severe social problems: they were withdrawn, fearful and anxious. Some were silent, as their early cries had received no response. They did not know how to play and withdrew from siblings and peers. This shows the effects of severe environmental neglect on children.

It is how children are looked after from day to day that has the most bearing on how children turn out. The above situation was an extreme one, but families in affluent Western societies are often under stress too. Depression in parents is increasing and marriage break-up rates are high. These stresses can have significant effects on children. Severely depressed parents will have less energy for their children and be more irritable. They will also be more likely to give in to their child's tantrums, as they do not have the strength to resist. Parents with severe relationship problems are also more stressed than others, and their children witness more arguments, shouting and uncertainty than other children do.

Many of the Romanian refugees were adopted by caring Canadian families, and Canadian researchers have followed their progress. These children had spent between eight months and four years in the orphanages before being adopted. Now most are twelve or thirteen years old.

Most of the medical problems (except Hepatitis B) are no longer a concern. The developmental delays, which were so severe, are greatly improved. When the children were first adopted they would lie quietly in bed without signalling to their parents that they had woken up. They had learned that no one would come. Once they realised that someone would come, their speech improved rapidly and they learned to communicate. A number of parents are still concerned about behavioural, social and emotional problems. The effects of such severe deprivation are hard to overcome. One can only shudder when one thinks of what would have happened to these children had they stayed in the orphanages. The children who improved most were those who spent least time in the orphanage. Just as importantly, the children adopted into the most nurturing and stimulating homes improved most and had fewer problems.

The environment in which a child is brought up has a major impact. Children inherit a certain temperament, but behaviour can be changed. Part 1 of this book shows how.

Recently there have been considerable advances in our understanding of how a child's brain develops in the early years. This has important implications for how we bring up our children. This research is described in the Appendix.

In a nutshell

- Children are born with very different temperaments.
- Although a child's inborn nature is important, the family environment in which he is brought up can be even more important.
- Child behaviour difficulties usually start off with a child having a very difficult or anxious nature.
- The way a parent interacts and manages the child's challenging nature then determines how the child will grow up.
- If there is a lot of family stress, it is likely to be more difficult for the parents to manage the behaviour in a positive way.

Part 1

Changing your child's behaviour

Cooperative behaviour is the most fundamental social skill. Most children who have behavioural difficulties at school started practising their defiance and disobedience at home. Cooperation affects how children learn at home and school.

A child's first and most important relationships are with her family. It is in the family that the child learns how to interact with others. She will carry this style over to her relationships with other people, particularly her peers and teachers.

Children who grow up to be cooperative and to have good social skills come from families where the parent–child relationships are positive. Children with difficult temperaments can put a great strain on parent–child relationships — their parents have to work harder to keep the relationship positive.

This section describes how parents can build stronger relationships with their children and encourage a cooperative attitude.

Taming the monster within

Parents often find themselves battling with their child, whether it is about their stubborn shyness or their defiance or tantrums. It sometimes becomes an 'Us versus Them' situation. When we start thinking of the child as a problem, the parent–child relationship starts to deteriorate. An effective way to shortcut this is to separate the problem from the child by 'objectifying' the problem. This involves making the problem an object, such as a monster, which is separate from the child. This technique works very well for children four years and above and children usually enjoy this part. It takes a bit to grasp, but if you follow the steps below it can be fun — as well as leading to fast improvements. These techniques come from an Australian therapist, Michael White, and a New Zealand therapist, David Epston, and are now used widely throughout the world.

Separate the child from the problem

The problem can be anything. It can be fear, anxiety, tantrums, aggressive behaviour, food refusal. The first thing to do is to sit down with your child and start to talk in a simple way, *against* the problem. Talk as though the problem is completely different from the child.

> 'Look Jeff, I'm a bit worried lately about your fear when it comes to going to preschool. Every morning it makes you cry and fight me when I try to get you ready. This fear is really making things difficult for you.'

> 'Jessica, I'm worried about these tantrums inside you. Sometimes they seem to get hold of you and make you angry and upset. I know you don't want to be like that, but it is as if the tantrums take you over.'

> 'Kristy, it seems like there is something inside you telling you not to eat. It makes you go so slowly at mealtimes. It seems to make you so upset.'

Give the problem a name

That is the first step: separate the problem from the child and isolate the *problem* as being the problem, not the child. When you have done this, it is important to get your child to give the problem a name. The idea is that the problem is not good for the child and needs a silly or nasty name. Monster names are often favourites with children. Names that children have given their problems are:

> 'Gollum' (from *Lord of the Rings*)

'He who shall not be named' (from the *Harry Potter* books and movies)

'Voldemort' (*Harry Potter*)

'The deadly anger'

'Silly fear'

'Scary monster'

'Nightmare troll'

'Tantrum monster'

'Sneaky wee or poo'

'Silly monster'

Once your child has found a name, get her to sit down and draw the 'problem'. While she is drawing it, ask her about all the ways it is making things bad for her:

1   Is it making her miserable?
2   Is it getting her into trouble?
3   Is it making her scared?
4   Does it make her do things she does not want to do?

The idea is to make the monster the baddie, not the child. Then the whole family can join forces *with* the child *against* the monster. From now on, do not discuss the problem using the child's name; discuss it only using the name the child has given it.

Battle tactics

The next step is to work out some tactics to defeat the monster (or whatever your child has decided to call it). It might help for your child to recall a time (if she is able) when the monster tried to take over, but she beat it. If she cannot remember one, try to remember a situation where you thought that the monster would take over, but your child actually resisted. For example, perhaps your child lost something, and instead of carrying on for three hours, only got a bit upset (and only carried on for two hours fifty-nine minutes — just joking!), then calmed down. Use this example to show your child that the monster can be beaten. In fact, now is the time to tell the child that the mon- **... separate the problem from the child and isolate the *problem* as being the problem, not the child.** ster may seem big, but is in fact incredibly stupid. It can be outsmarted easily and everyone in the family will help. Here are some examples.

Tantrum monsters

Tantrum monsters can make lots of trouble for children. There are a few things tantrum monsters do not like. One thing they really do not like is if the child and her parents are having fun. The next chapter shows how to set up a fun, con-flict-free time each day. Another thing the monster really hates is if when the child is upset, she goes into her own room. This is a good way of explaining to your child the strategy of time-out discussed in Chapter 7. So if your child feels the tan-trum monster coming on, she can go to her own room. It's her room, so she has more control over the monster there.

Fear monsters

Fear monsters tell children not to do things. Not to get ready for school. Not to go into the dark. Not to eat food. Fear mon-sters hate four things:

1   They hate it when the child is relaxed and happy
    (see Chapter 14 for relaxation exercises).

2   They hate it when the child uses positive self-talk
    (see Chapter 15).

3   They hate it when they are being ignored. If the fear
    monster tells a child not to do something — go into a
    room that is dark, for instance — the fear monster
    hates it when the child ignores him and goes into the
    room.

4   They hate it when Mum and Dad encourage the child
    for being brave (Chapter 5).

So, little by little, fear monsters can be defeated.

Nightmare monsters

Doris Brett, in her book *Annie Stories*, describes how children
can protect themselves in a nightmare using an invisible

magic ring. If you slip on the ring every night before you go to sleep, the nightmares cannot hurt you. It's a magic ring and it's invisible, so you cannot see it. The monsters in your dream may still come, but if you are wearing the ring, they cannot hurt you. In fact the nightmare monsters lose all their power and become really silly. So silly that they are easy to scare away if you just say 'Boo' in your sleep.

The other way you can all join together to beat nightmare monsters is to use the fact that they are not very smart and are easily caught. Help your child decorate a cardboard box. You can make it into a nightmare box with a very small hole in the top. Put an arrow saying 'Nightmare monsters this way' pointing towards the hole. Tell your child that nightmare monsters are so stupid that they follow the sign and go through the hole into the box. Then they are not smart enough to find their way out, so they get trapped for the whole night. In the morning you can seal up the box and throw them away.

Wee or poo monsters

Wee or poo monsters love it when children are absorbed in play and are a long way from the toilet. Wee and poo monsters are very sneaky like that. They can be beaten easily if for a week the child practises sprinting to the toilet. Parents can time how long it takes for a child to race to the toilet when they say 'Ready, set, go', just like in the Olympics.

Wee or poo monsters hate the toilet. The more often a child goes to the toilet, the more easily they are defeated. They also hate it if Mum and Dad praise the child for using the toilet.

Victories and defeats

The idea is that each time your child has a victory over the monster, that monster becomes weaker, until eventually it runs away. Talk to your child about how sneaky the monsters are: they sneak up on you and try to take over — each time they do this, you must be victorious.

Make up a chart of victories and defeats (see below). Your child will need some help filling it in. It should be a register of times when the monster tried to take over, but your child was victorious over it. If you notice times when your child might normally throw a tantrum or become anxious, but conquers the feeling, for instance, count that as a victory and help the child fill in the chart. For young children (under fives), just put a star on for victories. If the monster wins, record this as a defeat.

IMPORTANT: record victories as soon as possible, but wait until your child has calmed down before you record a defeat. Then you can discuss calmly how your child might win against the monster next time.

Victories	Defeats
Today I lost my ball and felt the tantrum monster creep up on me. I got a bit upset, but went to my room and calmed down.	I had a fight with my brother today. The tantrum monster won. I'll be ready for it next time and I'll take myself off to my room. It doesn't like that.
My brother picked on me and the tantrum monster did not like it when I walked away.	
Mum told me to get in the bath. The tantrum monster told me 'No' but I ignored him.	

Count up and talk about the victories. Tell your child that she is beating the monster so much that it is getting weaker and weaker.

Your child is not alone against the monster

Emphasise that your child is not alone in the battle against the monster. You and all the family are on her side. The odds are against the monster. Use the techniques in Chapter 5 to encourage your child to fight the monster. You might even want to use rewards every time your child is victorious against the monster. This can be very useful while you are encouraging your child to overcome her problems.

Every now and again you can try to gauge how powerful the monster is. You can do this in a number of ways:

- Draw a simple picture of your child and ask her to colour in how much of herself she thinks is taken over by the monster. Do this every week to see how much it lessens.
- When you talk about the monster, ask how big he is. Hold your hands apart and ask, 'Is he this big, or this big?' Check how big the monster is every week.
- Ask your child how strong the monster is. Draw a scale from 0–10, with 0 being very weak and 10 being incredibly strong. See each week how the monster's strength diminishes.

Other chapters in the book will give ideas on how 'the monster' can be defeated. The approach of using a monster is a useful tool because it places you and your child together against the monster. This is much better than you versus your child. It is also more likely to result in your child cooperating.

In a nutshell

- Objectify the problem by asking your child to give it a name.
- From then on, talk about the problem only by that name.
- Work out some battle tactics — think of as many ways as you can to beat the monster.
- Join forces with your child against the monster.
- Record victories and defeats.

Using play
to help your child

'Play is a child's work.' Maria Montessori

I was washing the car, and as is usual in today's world, I had lots of things to do and was in a hurry. It was then that my four-year-old uttered the three words that fathers dread most:

'Can I help?'

I was hoping to finish the same day, or at least before Christmas, but this was not to be. Of course he took the hose and within minutes I was soaked right through. The car, however, was still pretty dry and still dirty. I knew I was in a no-win situation. Best to just give up.

'Do you want a game of soccer?' I asked, thinking that at least I would be dry.

'Not now, Dad, I'm working,' said Martin.

Play is recognised as being an important way to teach an array of skills. Children learn to take turns through play, they practise fine and gross motor skills, they learn language, and they learn to use their imagination. Play can also be used to turn around relationships between parents and children.

It is all too easy for relationships between parents and their children to go downhill. Your child will not do as he is told. He digs his heels in over the tiniest thing. You get frustrated and angry. If this happens day after day, it becomes, 'Oh no, here we go again.'

You are caught in a vicious cycle. Your child becomes more and more negative, and so do you. The positive, enjoyable times become fewer and fewer. As you become less positive towards your child, he tries to get attention in other ways (not usually good ways).

Children get around four times more attention for negative behaviour than for positive behaviour. If a child were to pick up his toys straight away, probably all the attention he would get would be: 'That's a good boy.'

He gets far more attention by being disobedient. Children like to be the focus of attention, and being difficult is a very good way to have parents focus on you — even if it is negative attention.

Children can also get negative attention by getting upset or anxious. If a child starts crying when playing with other children, parents may remove the child and comfort him. This can then become a pattern in later life. We have all seen a child (and probably an adult) on the soccer field who falls over shrieking and writhing in agony when another player has merely brushed his shirt. He gets comforted, says he thinks he might be able to play on, gets a penalty and minutes later is running around as if nothing happened.

Some ancient societies were very advanced in their thinking about play. In ancient Greece, childhood was seen as an important preparation for the future. Plato said, 'It is in infancy that the whole character is effectively determined.' Play was seen as an important preparation for adult activities.

However, children were also seen as difficult to control, unruly, and in need of discipline — much like today.

There were other commonalities with our times. Some societies, such as ancient Rome, had similar social issues to ours. The divorce rate was high and remarriages occurred frequently. Men were away at war for long periods of time (they could not just hop on a jet and come home for some R&R). This led to more affairs and marriage breakdowns. Blended families were quite common and family life often became very complicated.

Child's Play

Child's Play is a way of playing that helps improve the relationship between you and your child. It is all too easy to focus on the negative behaviours of children. Child's Play helps focus on the positive. This is done by introducing a regular special time that is positive and enjoyable for both parent and child. This is the first step to building a stronger relationship. Gradually, as these positive interactions become more frequent, the relationship will improve.

Children get around four times more attention for negative behaviour than for positive behaviour.

A recent study showed that children whose parents interacted with them in this way were seen by other children as being more friendly. Teachers also rated the children as more helpful, cooperative and empathic.

The idea of Child's Play is to play with your child in a certain way. It is in fact derived from techniques of play therapy used by psychologists with children. If you took your child to a play therapist they could charge $150 per hour for this. DIY is cheaper, and with a bit of practice it's not too difficult.

There are a number of benefits of Child's Play:

- It is designed to give you a conflict-free time each day: no arguments, no shouting, no tantrums.
- It will also show you a special way of giving attention to your child that you can use to attend to your child's positive behaviour.
- After a while (about two weeks), Child's Play helps your child play imaginatively and more independently, with less need for parental guidance.
- Some parents report that it has a calming effect on their child, and almost all report that their child enjoys it.

How to do Child's Play

- Practise Child's Play at least once a day for 10 minutes.
- You can just join in with whatever he is doing. Alternatively, you can select several toys your child enjoys playing with. Your child is allowed to play with the toys in any way he likes, within reason.
- Say to your child something like 'Let's have our special play now.'

Don't

First we'll list the don'ts. This is the hard bit, learning not to do all the things that you often do in play. You will make mistakes, but try hard to keep to the following rules.

No questions

Try not to ask too many questions during Child's Play. Questions distract children from their play. And if you keep on interrupting the play with 'What are you doing now?', 'What is that a drawing of?', 'What colour is that?', 'How many blocks in that tower?', you are actually teaching your child to be distractable. Child's Play should not be a teaching exercise; it should be a relaxing and non-demanding time for you and your child.

This is not easy, because most parents get into the habit of asking questions all the time.

No instructions

Some children rely on their parents to guide them and give them instructions on what to do next — they seem unable to play on their own. Parents who try to direct their children by suggesting activities or giving instructions (such as 'Let's make a house', or 'Why don't you build a big road to the doll's house?') can actually increase this dependence.

Although a few instructions may be necessary to get the game started — 'Let's do some drawing', for instance — try to use as few instructions as possible during Child's Play.

No praise

Praise can be a very powerful tool. Some ways of praising children are more effective than others. Using praise effectively will be discussed in the next chapter.

In order to learn the skill of paying attention to your child's positive behaviour using the running commentary (see below), at this stage it is best to avoid using praise during Child's Play.

Mothers usually find it hard not to ask questions because they like to teach their children during play. Fathers find it hardest to not give instructions, because if fathers see something being done differently from how *they* think it should be done, they have trouble holding back.

(A recent study in the UK found that many children did not like playing with their fathers because the fathers always liked to win. I must say that this is not my experience — I find most children love to play with their dads. But dads, if you have to prove yourself by beating a seven-year-old, stop for a minute and think about their self-esteem, not yours.)

Western societies have not always appreciated the importance of play. We sometimes hear or read about times past that sound as if all families did was live the simple life together, with lots of spare time for family cohesion. Sons supposedly spent quality time with their father learning a trade and achieving male bonding. It was not always the case.

Before the eighteenth century, families consisted principally of parents with children under the age of seven or eight. Above that age a child became a working member of society or was apprenticed to a master to learn work skills. Families were large because almost half the children could be expected to die before they reached adulthood.

With the onset of the industrial revolution, many children suffered terribly. Worst off were the poorhouse children who did not have families to look after them. Poor children as young as six or seven worked sixteen or eighteen hour days in textile mills. They were sought after for the spinning wheel or the loom, because their quick, dexterous fingers could work faster than adults' fingers could (much as they are better at PlayStations in our age). Apart from the half-hour breakfast and lunch breaks, they were not allowed to go to the toilet or get a drink. Children who left their stations were whipped. Children were also used in mines, because they could get through smaller gaps than adults could. Vacations did not exist. Many children died in their teens, literally of overwork.

The recognition of childhood as a preparation for the future grew in the nineteenth century in Western society. Parents started to look at childhood as an investment in the child's later life. Play started to be seen as an essential part of growth and development.

Do

So what is the parent allowed to do during Child's Play? The following instructions sound easy, and as you read them you will probably think, *I do that anyway.* In practice, however, it is not as easy as it sounds. It will seem awkward at first, but with practice it will become easier and more natural.

Running commentary

- Describe enthusiastically what your child is doing. Imagine you are doing a commentary in a tennis, netball, cricket or football match.

- It might go something like this:

  'You've put the red block on the blue block, and now you're
  looking for another block. You're building a big tower and
  you're playing so nicely. Oh dear! They've all fallen down.
  Crash!'

- For younger children (under four), the running commentary should be fairly continuous and you should talk for most of the time. For children four years and above, comment less frequently on what they are doing.

- Child's Play is a time when your child can use his imagination. Your job is to show that you are interested by being there. Watching and commenting lets him know that you are paying attention.

- It is very difficult not to ask questions and not give instructions. Instead of asking questions, such as, 'What are you drawing?', turn it into a statement: 'You are drawing so carefully, what lovely colours!'

- Remember, make it enthusiastic and fun. Smile and look happy. It might feel awkward at first, but it does get easier with practice.

Examples of running commentary

'That's such a beautiful drawing — look at all those lovely colours.'

'I am wondering what you are making? You are putting those blocks together so carefully.'

'You're racing the cars: the red one is winning, now the blue one. They're going so fast.'

'You are making a road in the sand. It's a very long road. Now it's going through a tunnel.'

Tailgating

- Tailgating means staying close to your child — imagine you are tied to your child by a short length of rope.
- If your child is playing on the floor, get down on the floor yourself. If he is sitting at the table, sit next to him. If your child runs into another room, follow. If your child is running around in the garden, run with him.

Participation

- Be careful not to take over the game or allow your child to make you do everything. It is the Child's Play, not yours.
- You can join in by imitating what your child does, or by taking turns when your child offers. For example, you might pick up some playdough and roll it with him.

Concluding Child's Play

During Child's Play you are giving your child your complete attention, and he might not like it when you stop. It is a good idea to plan something else to go on to after Child's Play —

afternoon tea, outside play, a favourite television program. Prepare your child for the next activity. For example, you might say, 'It's nearly time for afternoon tea. We'll have to stop playing soon.'

> Enil was four years old and was close to being 'asked to leave' preschool. He regularly knocked over other children's toys and up-ended the craft table. He managed to scale the child-proof fence with ease and he kicked staff (including me when I was observing him). His coup d'état was when he got into the preschool office and took a large box of thumbtacks. He then tipped them out into the sandpit where many of the children were kneeling or playing in bare feet. Ouch.
>
> His behaviour at home was very disruptive. He had rolled the dog in builder's glue and poured flour over him. His parents were naturally extremely worried, and annoyed at Enil. His mother told me that she still loved him but reluctantly admitted that often she did not like him very much. I advised her to use Child's Play, followed by the other techniques used in the next three chapters. Gradually Enil's behaviour improved, but what was most gratifying was that he was so much happier and more affectionate towards his parents. Previously he wriggled away from any physical contact. Now he often came up to his mum or dad for a cuddle.

Possible problems

Some children might find the running commentary odd, and might say something like, 'Why are you talking like that?' If this happens, just say, 'I'm interested in what you're doing.' Children really enjoy the running commentary once they get used to it.

As your child is getting your full attention during Child's Play, it is unlikely that he will misbehave. If your child does display difficult or inappropriate behaviour during Child's Play, just say, 'If you don't play nicely I won't play with you.' If your child does not settle down quickly, say, 'You're not playing nicely, so I'm not playing any more' and leave the room. Try again later in the day.

It is best to play Child's Play with one child at a time. Of course this is not always possible, so if you are doing it with more than one child, switch the running commentary from one child to the other.

If you are playing Child's Play with more than one child and one is being negative, ignore the child who is displaying difficult behaviour. Shift your attention to the cooperative child and comment on what he is doing.

Using this skill at home

- Child's Play should be used at least five times a week. If possible, make it part of the daily routine.
- Make a record of each Child's Play session on a special record sheet (see example below).
- Remember, it takes a while to change behaviour. Give it at least two weeks and then, if you think it is helpful, make it a regular part of your day.
- You will make mistakes and inadvertently ask a few questions, give a few instructions or praise. Often the odd instruction is necessary to get the game going or if your child is stuck. However, it is important to keep these to a minimum. To see how you are doing, it might be a good idea to tape-record a session of Child's Play

and then play it back to make sure you are doing it correctly.

- Remember that practising Child's Play is laying the groundwork for a more positive interaction. The more positive the relationship between you and your child, the more effective any form of discipline will be.

Record of Child Play sessions

Date	How long did you play?	Did your child enjoy it?	How much did you use the running commentary?	Did you manage to avoid the Don'ts (see above) most of the time?

In one study in Atlanta, Georgia, a group of parents sought help for their very difficult preschool children. The children were highly disobedient and aggressive, so much so that it was expected that the problems would continue into the teenage years. The parents were taught skills such as Child's Play and time-out (as described in Chapter 7). The children were then followed up 14 years later and were found to have no more problems than any other children. It was thought that if they had not received help, they would have had far more delinquency problems and arrests than other children.

In a nutshell

- A regular time for playing with your child can help maintain a positive relationship.
- During Child's Play, ask as few questions as possible, give as few directions as possible, and give as little praise as possible.
- Practise the running commentary.
- Keep a record of your Child's Play sessions, so you can assess how well the sessions (and you!) are working.

Encouraging your child

Child's Play should gradually help strengthen the positive relationship between you and your child. After a while the running commentary will come easily and naturally. While still making time for Child's Play, try to use the running commentary style of attending to your child throughout the day. Take notice whenever your child is trying hard or has been playing for a while without bothering you. Just go up and attend to what she is doing for a few minutes, using the running commentary. At first this might backfire and your child might want more attention as soon as you go to leave. If you do this regularly, however, she will get to know that you are coming back and she will let you go.

Use the commentary at other times, too. If you are at the shops, just comment on the fact that your child is keeping close to you and helping with the shopping. When you have visitors, don't forget to break off from your conversation every now and again to go and see what your child is doing. Although this may sound tedious, it will let your child know that you have not abandoned her altogether and you will be coming back. This is better than your child doing the interrupting.

Use the running commentary as much as you can throughout the day. If you have a shy child, use it to encourage her in social situations. If the shopkeeper greets your child with, 'Hello Sally', your child might not reply, but you can still say, 'I'm glad you looked at Kevin when he said hello.' If your shy child is playing with other children, just go up and let her know you have noticed.

As we all know, it is very easy to get into a negative cycle when a child is going through a 'difficult' stage. The whole aim of these early chapters is to shift the balance so that your child gets more attention for positive behaviour than for difficult or shy behaviour. In this way you will be helping your child develop coping patterns of behaviour rather than negative, self-destructive behaviours. As your child's behaviour becomes more positive and you let her know you are pleased, your relationship will also become stronger.

Sometimes behaviour becomes so entrenched that a little extra is needed to shift it. Rewards can help — and they have the advantage that, unlike punishment, they are positive. There are two main types of reward:

1   social rewards, such as praise and encouragement
2   special rewards, which can be either activities your child enjoys (for example, going to the park, playing a game) or material rewards (for example, buying your child an ice cream or small treat).

Before we discuss these in detail, rewards have come in for some criticism in recent times. Let us briefly look at the arguments for and against rewards.

Do rewards harm children?

According to some authors, using praise and rewards is harmful to children. These writers argue that praising children makes them dependent on other people's opinions. They argue that praise leads children to do things only to please others, and that if you use rewards, your child will become a perfectionist with no in-built self-motivation. This, it is claimed, will lead to low self-esteem and poor schoolwork. No wonder parents are confused!

It seems that much of what these critics say is based on opinion only. The factual basis for these claims is questionable. In fact for some of the claims, such as that rewards make children dependent on external motivators and therefore reduce self-motivation, they are quite mistaken. Let's look at some of these claims in more detail.

Claims	What we know
Using rewards is bribery.	Bribes are used to get someone to do something *wrong* or *illegal*. Rewards are used to encourage your child to cooperate; this will help her at home and school.
Praise and rewards should not be used. If a child is only rewarded when she does something good, it will make her a perfectionist. Only encouragement should be used.	It is true that if a child is only praised or rewarded when she does something perfect, this sets standards that are too high. However, most parents praise children for making an effort, not for perfect performance. In this book, I argue that praise for trying hard is best, as it is more likely to help your child persist and do her best. This is what we all want from our children. This is encouragement. Praise and rewards can be used to encourage children.

	It is not praising in itself that is wrong, but *when* you praise can cause problems. Praise for effort, NOT for perfect performance.
Rewards reduce a child's self-motivation. Praise and other rewards make children dependent on others' opinion. They will always be looking for others' approval or a reward from someone else. This decreases self-esteem and leads to poor schoolwork.	There is little evidence for this. Praise and other rewards help children learn new skills and also motivate children to perform tasks they are reluctant to do. As the skill is learned, we gradually reduce the external rewards and praise. Self-motivation then takes over. There is abundant evidence for this.
Children should do as they are told without rewards. If we reward them they will expect a reward for doing everything.	It is true that if you give your child treats a lot she will expect it for other things. Treats should be used for very specific behaviours, such as to encourage your child if she is having difficulty learning something. Then, when she has got the hang of it, the treats should be phased out.

Rewards are part of life. Would you go to work if you were not paid? We can safely say that praise and rewards, used in moderation (too much can cause big heads), are generally beneficial. Praise given as *encouragement*, that is, praising children for giving something their best shot and sticking at a task — 'You've tried really hard at that puzzle', for instance — is very effective. Praise for perfect performance or comparing with other children — 'You are the best helper in the class', for example — is not a good idea, as it can lead to anxiety. It is effort we want to reward, so that children learn to do their best.

Having looked at the pros and cons of rewards, let's now discuss the two types of reward in more detail.

Social rewards (praise)

We discussed in the previous chapter how to use a running commentary. This is the best way to encourage children. It can be used frequently during the day to show children that you have noticed their good behaviour. However, we should praise children for special efforts, of course, and tell them how proud we are. Praise is a little bit like the icing on a cake. No icing — boring, dry cake. Too much icing — sickly cake.

Some ways of praising are better than others. The most common way we praise children is by saying things like 'Good girl' or 'Well done.' This is called *unlabelled praise*, and is the least effective way of praising children. It is not very effective because it does not specify or label exactly what you are pleased with.

Labelled praise, on the other hand, involves telling your child exactly what you were pleased with. An example of labelled praise might be, 'You've worked so hard on that drawing — it looks lovely.' There are more examples below.

Labelled praise is more effective than unlabelled praise for a number of reasons. First, it is just that bit more special and lets your child know that you really have noticed her. Second, we have talked about the fact that we need to give children more attention for positive behaviour. 'Good girl' lasts all of one or two seconds. 'You're a good girl for getting dressed all by yourself. Well done!' is much more beneficial.

Examples of labelled praise

'It was so good of you to play quietly while I was on the phone. Thank you.'

'That's a beautiful drawing. What lovely colours! You are clever!'

'You are a good girl for brushing your teeth so well.'

'Your teacher told me how well you are doing at school and how enthusiastic you are about learning. I'm so proud of you!'

'You've been playing with that Lego for ages. I know it all collapsed before, but you are such a good girl for not getting angry. You stuck at it.'

'Thanks for helping your brother. You are a good girl.'

'I noticed that you walked away when your brother got very angry and started hitting you. You didn't hit back. That was a very grown-up thing to do. Well done!'

It's not what you say, it's the way that you say it

A friend of mine has a son, Brett, who is two and a half, and was a little concerned about his lack of progress with toilet training. Brett just did not seem in the least interested, and he was obviously not as anxious as his parents were that he was still in nappies. So one day, as many parents do, his dad went with him to the toilet to show him how to do a wee (after all, modelling is the best way of teaching, right?). Fully confident of immediate results, Dad demonstrated. Brett looked on bemused, obviously a little unsure of what this was all about. When Dad had finished, Brett looked up and said very enthusiastically, 'Well done, Dad, good onya!'

Then he just walked out without even thinking of making an attempt himself.

Psychologists have found that when you are giving a message to a child, such as, 'I am pleased with you', the actual words you say convey only about 7 percent of the meaning. The other 93 percent of the meaning is conveyed by your tone of voice and your body language. In other words, if you say, 'That's fantastic' in a bored, tired monotone from across the room, your child will probably decide that you do not really mean it.

Giving a positive message to your child is about saying the right thing — using the running commentary or labelled praise — and about how you say it. If you sound enthusiastic and interested, that will emphasise the message. If you show through your body language that you are pleased, it will make all the difference. Get close to your child, give her a big smile and a pat or a hug. Children pick up on body language more quickly than adults.

Special rewards

It is true that if special rewards are overused it does set up an expectation. The next time you ask your child to do something, she might reply, 'What do I get?'

Special rewards can, however, be used briefly for turning a specific behaviour around. For example, if your children are fighting all the time, giving a reward for periods when they get along together can help. Special rewards must be very specific. If the child knows the reward is only for one thing, she will not expect it for other things.

Reward systems should be a temporary solution. If they do not work quickly, something is wrong with the way they are being used. If you follow the instructions below, they should work. After a few weeks you should phase out the rewards.

Reward systems work for children three years and over. For children aged nine or over, money can work wonders, although for a few children it does not mean much. This is one of the tricks of rewarding — the reward has to be important to the child. There are other important tricks, too. Let us go through them one by one.

One behaviour at a time

Start with only one behaviour at a time. If you have more than one child, use a reward system for each child. It is important to involve your child in any reward system. This is a negotiation; you are asking your child to do something *you* want, and in exchange she gets something *she* wants. Everyone benefits.

> Giving a positive message to your child is about saying the right thing ... and about how you say it.

The first thing to do is explain what you want your child to do. Be very specific. For example, if you have a shy child you might want her to play with visitors when they arrive rather than hanging off your coat. Or you may just want her to say hello to your friend's children. With shy or anxious children, make sure you are not asking too much. For example, if they do not feel they can say hello, ask them if they can give a wave or a smile instead. There is no point promising rewards if the task is too hard for your child.

For children with challenging behaviour, just choose one situation, such as picking up toys or playing nicely with her brother for a short time. The time depends on the child's age: it might only be a few minutes for young children (up to five), and up to 20 minutes for older children. It must be specific and easy at first. A goal of 'Being good for a week' is doomed to failure.

Write down what you want your child to do. It is important to write it as a 'Please do', not as a 'Don't'.

Rather than, 'Stop being noisy while I am on the telephone', it is better to write, 'Play quietly while I am on the telephone.'

Here are some examples:

- doing chores, such as picking up toys after play
- tidying room every day
- making bed
- feeding pets
- good mealtime behaviour (sitting at table, eating and not disrupting)
- playing nicely with brother or sister for 20 minutes
- playing quietly while Mum or Dad is on the telephone
- saying nice things to brother or sister
- getting dressed
- getting ready for school or preschool on time
- brushing teeth
- going to have a bath as soon as asked
- not interrupting while Mum and Dad are talking (or watching the news)
- playing with other children who come to visit: sharing and taking turns with them
- keeping calm when things go wrong (when a toy is broken, for instance).

Negotiating rewards

Next, negotiate the rewards. Go through the list opposite with your child and find out which rewards she likes most. It does not have to be *buying* something for her (material reward). Mostly, it is better if it is *doing* something with her (activity reward), such as playing a game or taking her down to play in the park.

There are two important things about this process of negotiation that you must remember:

1   First, if you have discussed rewards and your child has earned a reward, it is very important that you fulfil your part of the bargain. When I ask some parents if their child got a reward, they say, 'Oh, I forgot' or 'She didn't ask for one.' Then they wonder why it did not work.

2   You choose which rewards you are prepared to give. You might not have time to take your child to the pool, so offer a choice of other rewards that you can give more easily.

Go through the list and ask your child if she **Likes it a lot, Likes it a bit,** or **Does not like it at all.**

Each time your child earns a reward (see chart on page 58), select one and give it to your child **as soon as possible.**

Reward list			
Everyday rewards	**Like a lot**	**Like a bit**	**Do not like**
Hug			
Game with Mum or Dad			
Story from Mum or Dad			
Going for a walk			
Going to the park			
Drawing or painting			
Riding bike			
Watching favourite TV program			

Money			
Board game (Cluedo, Monopoly)			
Favourite snacks — fruit, cake, chocolate, ice cream			
Cooking with Mum or Dad			
Having a friend over to play			
Going out for morning or afternoon tea			
Playing a ball game (netball, soccer)			
Playing computer games			
Making something			
Special rewards			
Going to see a friend			
Staying up late			
Watching a video/DVD			
Watching a movie			
Going to the beach or pool			
Going on a picnic			
Going on a bushwalk			
Getting a new book or small toy			
Visiting the library or museum			
Going fishing			
Going out to dinner			
Having a sleepover			

Important points about rewards

- **The rewards have to be special and different from what your child gets on a normal day.** If she gets chips whenever she wants, for example, she will not be motivated to earn them. Limit the rewards (apart from hugs) as much as possible so that they are special. It is the same with money. If you buy your children whatever they want, money will not mean much to them.

- **Give the rewards as soon as possible after your child has earned them.** If it is something you cannot give straight away, such as a trip to a museum or the beach, start planning it with your child straight away and talk about what you will do when you get there.
- **Vary the rewards as much as you can.** Children will quickly get bored if they get the same reward each time.
- **Using the chart on page 58, start off with everyday rewards.** You can save a special reward for the end or for special effort.
- **Don't forget to praise as well.** The praise can mean more to your child than the reward.

Reward chart

Use the chart illustrated on page 58. Each time your child has earned a reward use a stamp, stickers or just draw on the squares in the chart. Praise your child each time, and show her that you are marking the square on the chart. The blank squares mean that your child does not get a special reward. You must explain this to your child carefully.

When she gets a sticker on a blank square, make sure she gets lots of labelled praise and attention and hugs. Let her know that she is near a special surprise. When it is time to fill in a square with 'SURPRISE' on it, give a reward. Do this as soon as possible and don't forget to do it, or next time your child might 'forget' to behave.

There may be something that your child especially wants — this can be given for the very last surprise. Let your child know that this is what she will get when the entire chart is filled in.

The advantage of this chart is that at the start it is easy for your child to earn a reward. Gradually, as your child gets used to behaving more cooperatively, the rewards are not given as often. Over time the rewards are phased out.

An alternative reward chart can be used if there is something your child really wants, such as a special toy (which you were probably going to get her anyway). Draw a picture of the toy and then divide it up into a dozen or so segments (fewer for younger children, and more for older children who want something more expensive and are more able to wait for things). Each time your child completes the agreed behaviour, let her colour in one segment. (Keep this hidden between colourings, as the temptation often becomes too much and your child may colour it in when you are not watching!)

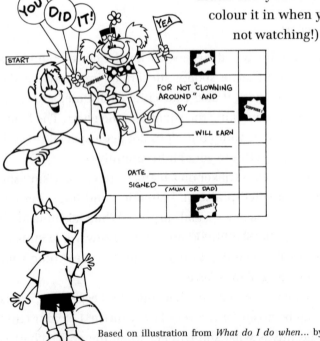

Based on illustration from *What do I do when...* by Juliet V. Allen. Reproduced with kind permission of Impact Publishers.

In a nutshell

- Praise and rewards are part of life and can be very beneficial.
- Praise used as encouragement for effort is better than praise that is only used when a child has completed something successfully.
- Material and activity rewards can be used temporarily to turn a behaviour around.
- Reward charts can be useful for encouraging cooperative behaviour.
- It is best to make the rewards easy to earn at first, rather than difficult — or unattainable.

Sending clear messages

How you ask your child to do something can make a huge difference to whether he will take notice. Many parents who have challenging children quickly become impatient and get out of control. Then who is in control? The child, of course.

How do children know that Mum or Dad is not in control? As we noted in the previous chapter, children pick up on body language better than most adults. They see parents become agitated, clench their jaws and wave their hands around. Many parents 'natter'. They talk fast, without a break, and go on and on and on and on and on … In fact there has been a fair bit of research on nattering. It has been found that nattering is very irritating to children, and makes their behaviour *worse*. As soon as a parent starts nattering, children whine more and their tantrums go on for longer. Exactly the opposite of what the parent wants. If parents natter, their children are much less likely to do as they are told and more likely to argue, answer back and dig their heels in.

The best training for how to look in control is to watch some movies with really cool actors. Some of the classics are best. Try Clint Eastwood in *Dirty Harry* or Sigourney Weaver in *Alien*. Watch how *they* handle conflict. The first thing to notice is that they do not natter. In fact they often do not say much at all, and what they do say is slow and measured. The 'Make my day' or 'I'll be back' were said in a level tone, totally unhurried. Another thing to notice is that they do not move around much. Their movements are slow and relaxed, as if they have all the time in the world. They do not jerk around excitedly. Lastly, when at a crucial stage in the power struggle, they fix their opposite number with a stare and do not flinch. Watch how they do it and practise being a movie star next time you have a conflict with your child.

It has been found that nattering is very irritating to children, and makes their behaviour *worse*.

Here are a few other tips that are important when giving instructions to children.

Gain your child's attention

Some children act deaf when you are trying to tell them something. To avoid this:

1 Stand in front of your child.
2 Say your child's name *first*. This will attract his attention. (If you give an instruction, such as 'Go and brush your teeth, Ben', Ben might only pay attention when he hears his name. He will have missed the instruction

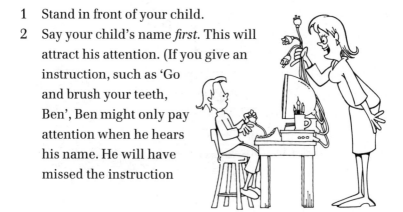

which came before. Saying 'Ben' first gains his attention so he will listen for the instruction.)

3   Make eye contact.

4   Then give an instruction.

Be brief, clear and specific

Try not to give long, vague instructions. Giving children
detailed explanations is important if you are asking your child
to do something for the first time. For example, if you are
showing your child for the first time how to use a computer,
you need to take your time and explain what to do and why.
Most instructions, however, are everyday things that you
have asked your child to do hundreds of times — they do not
require any further explanation. If you are asking him to get
into the bath, which is something you have asked for the last
five years, it is not necessary to give long explanations. Just
keep it short.

JACK, PLEASE
GO TO BED NOW.

'Jack, please get in the bath' is sufficient.

If your child says 'Why?' for something like this, it is often a stalling tactic; you should not feel guilty about replying, 'Because I said so.'

If you have a number of instructions to give, give them one at a time. Use positive attention each time your child cooperates, and then give the next instruction.

Don't ask

In these days of requiring consensus before doing anything, we have got into the habit of asking questions all the time. This is fine if you want to give your child a choice of what to do. Problems occur if you really want them to do something, like go to bed.

Then, 'Tim, darling, how would you like to stop watching television and go to bed?' will not do. He might just say, 'No, that's all right Mum, I'll do it later.'

Instead, give a clear direction. It does not have to be unpleasant; it just has to give the message that there is no choice, some things must be done.

'Tim, pack up your toys now please' is quite adequate and does not give a choice.

Another common mistake is to say 'Let's ...', such as, 'Let's pick up your toys.' Let's means 'let us', as in WE will pick up your toys. This is fine if you are going to do it together. Guess who will be doing most of the picking up.

Focus on the positive

Instructions that tell a child what *not* to do are quite ineffective.

'Stop arguing with me.'

'Stop fighting.'

'Don't be naughty.'

These instructions tell your child what you do not want him to do, but fail to give a clear message about how you want him to behave instead. It is much better when giving an instruction to let your child know exactly what you want him to do.

'Sean, please listen when I am speaking.'

'Sam and Alice, please take turns with the computer. I'll time you.'

'Jonathon, sit on the lounge — do not jump.'

These instructions are much clearer and tell your children exactly what you expect. Have a look at the following instructions and see if you can tell why the incorrect ones are wrong.

Incorrect instructions	Correct instructions
'Please pick up your toys, Laura.'	'Laura, please pick up your toys.'
'Ben, stop being a nuisance.'	'Ben, please play quietly while I'm on the phone.'
'Would you like to go to bed now, Jackie?'	'Jackie, please go to bed now.'
'Now can you pick up your toys? And when you've done that you can tidy up your room? And you left a lot of things outside, so you can bring them in?'	'Jodie, please pick up your toys … You've done such a good job, it's looking much tidier. Now, please pick up the clothes off the floor in your room … You're being such a good girl.'

Practice makes perfect

First of all, it is best to practise giving instructions when your child is most likely to cooperate. Wait for him to be in a good mood. Only ask for little things that do not require much effort and that you are fairly sure he will do. Here are some examples:

'Alice, please open the door for me.'

'Angus, pass me a tissue, please.'

'John, please pass that pencil over.'

'Kate, please let the dog out for me.'

While you are practising these instructions, be sure to use labelled praise as soon as your child cooperates. The idea is to set the situation up so that you give an instruction that is likely to be followed. You then give positive attention. This gradually changes the balance of interactions in a more positive direction. Rather than lots of negative interactions, you are setting up more positive ones.

In a nutshell

- Parent nattering makes behaviour worse.
- Gain your child's attention by saying his name first.
- When giving instructions be brief, clear and specific.
- Don't ask.
- Focus on the positive.
- Give your child very easy instructions that he is likely to cooperate with, such as, 'Phil, please pass me a tissue.' This gives you more opportunity to praise.

Dealing with disobedience

The rise in delinquency is often blamed on the lack of discipline in society in general today. The cane is no longer used in most schools in Western societies and, gradually, laws against parents smacking children are being introduced. The main reason for corporal punishment being legislated out is that in the past we have not always been good at protecting children. In England, the Royal Society for the Prevention of Cruelty to Animals was founded 60 years before a similar organisation was set up for children (the National Society for the Prevention of Cruelty to Children).

There is no doubt, looking at the history of child-rearing (see below), that previous generations had serious problems trying to control children's behaviour. Their attempts might be described as something like this:

1950s — ignore them

1960s — smack them

1970s — smack them lovingly

1980s — spoil them

1990s — do nothing: let them be their own person

2000s — ?

Today, discipline is still a major issue. Many teachers report that student behaviour is the number one problem in schools today.

What is the best way to deal with a child who is not doing as she is told? Should you ignore her, smack her, reason with her, give her love or try to help her solve the problem?

Psychologists often use the saying, 'It takes a village to raise a child.' This conjures up images of peaceful tribes and ancient cultures living in harmony with nature and children running around laughing while adults are always on hand to help and protect. While no doubt some cultures and tribes were enlightened, others were not. In Ancient Rome, fathers had the right to take the life of a newborn as well as their other children. They were, however, under some pressure to rear all sons (for war) and the first-born daughter (for future child-rearing). In many ancient cultures infanticide was practised, particularly if the baby was weak or deformed (or female). Abandonment was one way of dealing with 'problem children'.

In the eighteenth century, one way of keeping children 'on the straight and narrow' was to take them to public hangings. Sometimes this was a school excursion to educate children as to what would happen if they broke the law.

Discipline methods

Children misbehave for two main reasons:

1 First, most of our instructions concern doing things children do not want to do.

'Pick up your toys!'

'Stop playing and get dressed!'

'Turn the TV off and brush your teeth.'

Some children learn that by throwing a tantrum and making life as difficult as possible for parents, it is possible to get away with things. If they do get away with it, they will keep trying.

2   Second, children enjoy attention. You may think they already get a lot, but attention is a bit like money: no matter how much we have, we always want more.

As we saw in Chapter 4, children get around four times more attention for disobeying than they do for positive behaviour.

In the previous chapters we have looked at ways of increasing attention for positive behaviour, and at how to give correct instructions. These are the groundwork for this chapter. Any discipline method must take into account the above two points. The child must not get away with disobedience. Also, she must not get extra attention for lack of cooperation. Let us examine some common methods of discipline.

Explaining and reasoning

If your child is encountering a new situation and is not sure what to do, of course you should explain. Such as when we first took our daughter, then aged three, to the zoo — she tried to climb over into the bear enclosure because she thought they were cute. We had to explain (after calming ourselves down) that they were not like the bears in the cartoons.

Most day-to-day situations, however, do not need an explanation. For these familiar things, mostly you have already explained what is required a dozen times; there is no need for more. For some children, reasoning works quite well, but for others … well, they are simply sometimes not reasonable. Reasoning is also giving your child extra attention for difficult behaviour.

Discuss things with your child, certainly, but wait until she is calm and quiet. Trying to explain and reason while your child is in the middle of a tantrum is likely to fail. It often leads to an argument, which means that your child is probably getting away with not doing as she is told. Also, if you let a child argue with you all the time, you are really saying to them, 'I am no longer in control, you are.'

Many teachers report that student behaviour is the number one problem in schools today.

Nattering

We discussed nattering in Chapter 6. This is where you just go on and on and on and on and on …

'Look, I told you to pack your toys away. Why don't you do anything I say? You just sit there while I do everything for you and when I ask you to do the tiniest thing you won't do it. Well I'm not doing any more for you. That's it. And if you don't pick up those toys I'm never going to take you to the toyshop ever again …'

As we said, not only does nattering not work — it actually makes your child's behaviour worse. So I won't go on and on about it. Just try not to do it; you are wasting your breath.

Smacking

A friend was frustrated at his seven-year-old son's behaviour when they were at a picnic. His options were limited, as he could not send him to his room, so he threatened to give him a smack.

'But Dad!' came the reply. 'What's the point? It will only make me worse!'

Children often play up to get a reaction, and smacking is certainly a reaction. It often makes both you and your child upset. You feel guilty and your child is still crying (probably more). Also, children copy their parents. If you smack your child when you are angry or frustrated with her, you are teaching her that aggression is how you handle anger and frustration. The next time she is angry or upset with her sister or another child, she could well imitate your behaviour and use aggression. This is obviously not what is wanted.

Parents shout, yell and hit when they are angry. Anger can be a huge problem. It is a significant predictor of heart disease — it can be worse for your health than high cholesterol. It is a significant factor in family breakdown. Angry parents produce angry children, and angry children do not turn out healthy and well adjusted.

Screaming and shouting

Most parents today do not want to smack their children. It leaves an unpleasant feeling for a long time. Many parents are

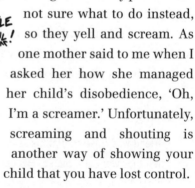

not sure what to do instead, so they yell and scream. As one mother said to me when I asked her how she managed her child's disobedience, 'Oh, I'm a screamer.' Unfortunately, screaming and shouting is another way of showing your child that you have lost control.

In fact, what is happening is that you are having a tantrum because your child is having a tantrum. Trying to get your child to control her temper by losing yours does not help the situation. Of course it also means that your child is the focus of attention.

You are the most important role model for your child. Children of all ages imitate their parents. If your child sees that when you get upset, you yell and shout, she will do the same thing.

I was doing some woodwork. Martin (aged three) was watching. I slipped with the saw and cut myself. I swore.

Martin: 'What?'

Dad: 'Oh, nothing, Daddy's just been naughty.'

Martin: 'That's all right, Dad, I'm naughty too!'

One easy way to remind yourself not to yell and scream is to wear an elastic band around your wrist. This should act as a reminder not to yell. If you hear yourself yell, scream or shout, give yourself a 'ping'. It hurts, but it is effective and will soon stop you.

Helping your child solve problems

We will cover problem solving in detail in Part 3. It certainly is an extremely important skill to teach young children (you can begin when they are about three, but you may have little success for a year or two). However, just as you do not teach your child maths or reading when she is having a tantrum, neither is it productive to teach problem solving at this time. Your child will be too upset to learn and you will be too stressed to teach her. It is sometimes possible to prompt problem solving if you think your child is *about* to have a tantrum or hit someone. If you can get in just before she chooses an aggressive or coercive behaviour, it might work. However, it is usually best to teach problem solving (like any other skill) when your child is calm.

Goals for change

Take a few minutes to ask yourself what you would like to change. First of all, what would you like to change about your own behaviour? Would you like to:

- reduce nattering?
- reduce screaming and shouting?
- reduce smacking?

Second, think about what you would like to change about your child's behaviour. Would you like to:

- reduce the aggressive behaviour and fighting?
- reduce the defiance and answering back?
- reduce the arguing?
- reduce the disobedience?
- reduce the tantrums?

Write down your goals on a piece of paper.

We will now look at some methods that can help you achieve your goals. The common problem with the methods of managing child behaviour that we have already mentioned is that they all give your child extra attention for misbehaviour. Does this mean that you should ignore negative behaviour? Well, maybe and maybe not.

Ignoring

Ignoring sounds easy, but in practice it can be quite hard to do. It is also *not* useful for aggressive behaviours or disobedience.

Ignoring is often recommended for fighting between siblings. However, siblings rarely sort things out by themselves if left to their own devices. Also, with siblings (except for twins), there is an age difference and therefore often a power imbalance. The stronger child wins almost all the time, learning that aggression pays. The younger or weaker child loses and becomes a lifelong victim, learning that there is no way she can win.

Ignoring is also unhelpful for disobedience. If you ask a child to pick up her toys and she does not, what happens if you ignore her? She still does not pick up her toys. She has managed to avoid doing what you asked.

So what is ignoring useful for? Attention-seeking behaviours such as temper tantrums and whining. Even for these behaviours, ignoring is not easy. For a start, when you are ignoring a behaviour such as a tantrum, the tantrum usually gets worse before it gets better. If you give attention or give in when it gets worse, all you have done is to teach your child that she must get louder before you give in. There are four main rules for ignoring:

1   Do not look at your child. It is best to turn your back or walk out of the room (as long as you are sure she will be safe).
2   Do not say anything. Do not keep telling her to stop.
3   Do not give any physical contact. In fact, keep your distance.

4   Start ignoring as soon as the tantrum begins. Continue ignoring until it stops. This is the most difficult part of ignoring, as the tantrum usually gets worse before it gets better. If your child starts doing something that is potentially harmful, go straight to time-out (see below).

Where you have more than one child at home, you will often find that when one child is having a tantrum, the other is well behaved. Yet, as parents, we often give all the attention to the one who is misbehaving. So we are teaching both children that throwing a tantrum gets attention, but behaving appropriately does not. Next time this happens, turn your back on the child having the tantrum and give all your attention to the child who is well behaved. Your tantrumming child will soon learn that every time she has a tantrum, you give attention to her sibling. Not at all what she wanted.

Time-out

If your child's main problems are disobedience or aggressive behaviour, time-out is the best alternative. Many parents will have heard of time-out and most would have tried it in one form or another. If it is to work properly, it must be done very systematically, as outlined below.

Time-out means a short period of time when your child is put in a place on her own so she can calm down. In time-out, your child is not given any positive attention from you. The time-out place should be boring. Time-out should be given for short periods of time. Longer periods are usually no more effective. It is better to use time-out ten times for brief periods than for one long period.

Choosing a time-out location

The main consideration when choosing a time-out place is that it should be as boring as possible. Your child should not get any attention, and should not be able to watch television or play interesting games.

The most common place for time-out is the child's bedroom. The main problem with this solution is that your child may play with her toys. Also, some children have TVs or Play-Stations in their rooms. One way around this is to remove their favourite toys while they are in time-out and remove any videogame software.

Other parents are concerned that using the bedroom will associate the bedroom with punishment. This may be true for children under two years old, but older children can tell the difference between being sent to the bedroom as punishment and going there at other times, such as at bedtime, to sleep.

If it is not possible to use the bedroom, you can use other rooms as long as they are safe. Not the bathroom, toilet or laundry — there are too many dangerous things in those rooms. The parents' bedroom is a possibility.

A chair in the hallway or by a wall is good if your child will stay there without a struggle. Make sure it is an adult-size chair so your child's feet cannot touch the ground. Then she will not be able to move the chair around so easily. In fact, sitting on a chair for a few minutes doing nothing is the *best* place for time-out, as it is really boring. However, if you have to fight to keep your child there, it defeats the purpose, as your child is still getting a lot of attention.

It is important to follow the time-out procedure outlined below carefully; if you don't, it will not work.

Step 1: Specify the behaviour

Specify exactly what time-out will be used for. Before time-out, it is best to go through the process of separating the behaviour from the child outlined in Chapter 3 (remember, this way of objectifying the problem can be used only for children four years and up). If your main problem is disobedience and tantrums, you might say time-out is for the 'tantrum monster' (or whatever name your child has chosen). If your child is aggressive, you may say that time-out is for the 'anger monster'. You can explain that those monsters do not like time-out. You can say that after a few minutes in time-out the 'monster' gets weak. Then it is easier to overcome the monster.

It is best to target aggressive behaviour or defiance at first. If your child is repeatedly aggressive, this is something you want to stop — it may become a pattern she takes to school. You may then need to work on the 'anger monster'. If your child is defiant, and argues and answers back, it means she is not respecting your authority. In this case you need to work on the 'arguing monster'.

If disobedience, not these behaviours, is of most concern, this too can be tackled with time-out, as will be seen below.

Red card offences

The most common error parents make when using time-out, or any discipline method, is that they give too many warnings. A useful way to avoid this mistake is to use the discipline method used in soccer. For serious offences a red card is used. No warnings are given, because the players already know exactly what offences are red card offences — punching an opponent, arguing with the referee, for instance. The player is then sent off. No ifs, no buts, no arguing. For other offences a yellow card is used. This is a warning card. Players get *one*, and *only* one, warning. If a player has been shown a yellow card, and he commits another offence, he automatically gets a red card.

There are two main red card offences for children:

1 aggressive behaviour
2 defiance (answering back).

Aggressive behaviour is a red card offence because it can be serious. Also, if you give warnings for aggression, the following pattern can occur:

> I was asked to see a particularly aggressive four-year-old, Tom, at preschool. At the slightest provocation (or sometimes with no provocation) he would hit, knock over blocks other children were building or throw things at others. He even kicked or spat at teachers.
>
> Whenever he was aggressive he would get a warning. He did not seem to take much notice of this; it seemed to deter him for a little while, but then he was aggressive again. He received another warning. Again he would wait for 20 minutes or so, and again he would be aggressive. He then received another warning. During the morning session I counted more than ten fairly serious acts of aggression and the same number of warnings. At no time did Tom receive any discipline. He was spoken to and warned. In fact he was getting extra attention. The warnings did not have any effect.

In soccer, if a player punches, kicks or spits at another player it is an automatic red card. This also works best for childhood aggression at home. That means your child goes straight to time-out (or the Sin Bin), with no warning.

If you have two children fighting, it is no use trying to find out who started it. You will get two entirely different opinions. Send both to time-out (in different places). Even if only one threw a punch, the other probably provoked it, so still send both.

The other red card offence in soccer is arguing with or abusing the referee. If this was not dealt with severely, the referee would lose control of the game. In the same way, defiance (arguing with Mum or Dad — the referee — or answering back) should be a red card offence at home. It should mean time-out straight away, with no warnings.

- Discuss the behaviours with your child and let her know that any aggression or answering back will immediately result in a red card and she will go straight to time-out (or the Sin Bin). Yes, she might think this is funny for the first one or two times, but that will wear off.
- You might put a list of the rules on her door. If she cannot yet read, draw some pictures.
- You can remind her of the rules first thing each morning for the first week. Then each time the behaviour occurs in the home (we will look later at how to deal with behaviours away from home), march your child off to the time-out room. For red card offences, NO WARNINGS ARE GIVEN.
- You can make up a red card with aggression and/or defiance and/or answering back (or anger monster, tantrum monster) written on it. The red card means that as soon as your child is taken over by the anger monster, she goes straight to time-out.
- Do not lecture. Just say something like, 'No, the anger monster has taken over, go to the time-out room.'

- If your child will not go, lead her there. If she is small enough, you can pick her up and carry her.

Yellow card offences

A yellow card is slightly more involved than a red card. It is mostly used for one very common behaviour: disobedience.

A yellow card is given as a warning. A second yellow card is equivalent to a red card, and means your child goes to time-out. This is how it works. Disobedience starts off with an instruction (make sure you get your instruction correct — see Chapter 6).

> 'Briony, please pick up your toys.'

Wait five seconds. If there is no response after five seconds, count this as a yellow card offence. Hold up the yellow card.

> 'Briony, if you do not pick up your toys you go straight to the time-out room.'

Wait five seconds. If your child still does not cooperate, hold up the red card and take your child to the time-out room.

If your child cooperates before the red card is shown, do not forget to praise. However, if you show the red card and your child then says, 'OK, I'll do it', it is too late. You must still use time-out.

Step 2: Use a timer

One of the most useful behaviour management devices is a kitchen timer. These are quite inexpensive, but very useful for implementing time-out. Set the timer outside the child's time-out room door so she can hear when the time is up.

One parent I worked with put her young child in time-out. An old friend of hers phoned and they talked for quite a long time. She then went back to cooking. It was a while before she wondered why her normally demanding preschooler had been so quiet. Then she remembered, he was in time-out. He'd been in time-out for over an hour. After this she made sure she bought a timer and put it outside the bedroom door so both she and her child could hear when the time was up.

The other reason a timer is useful is that it stops your child calling out, 'Can I come out now?' You make it clear that she has to wait for the timer to sound. Many children just wander out of time-out when they feel like it. If you have not set a time, they often get away with this. However, this means the child is in control of time-out, not you. By using a timer, it is clear how long the child must stay there. You are in control. It is very important to ignore any calling out or screaming while your child is in time-out.

How long should time-out be? A good guide is simply to use ONE minute for EACH YEAR of age. Otherwise, research suggests that four or five minutes is suitable for preschool children and primary school-aged children.

Tell your child that she can come out when she is quiet when the timer goes off.

Time-out can also be used very occasionally for toddlers (eighteen months to three years), but only for dangerous behaviour. If you are using the bedroom as the time-out room, put your toddler in for just one or two minutes. Leave the door open. If your toddler keeps coming out, put her back and close the door, but only very briefly — for 30 seconds or so. Then wait until she catches her breath, quickly open the door and say, 'Good, you're quiet, you can come out now.'

Step 3: Only let your child out when she is quiet

Your child is only allowed out when the timer goes off *if* she is quiet. If she is not quiet, she probably won't hear the timer anyway, so it's a good incentive to calm down.

If you let your child out before she has quietened down, the anger monster is still well and truly in control. Wait until the child is winning the battle against the anger monster, even if the anger monster has only paused for breath.

If your child is still crying or screaming loudly when the timer goes off, say something like: 'You may come out when you are quiet.' Then wait until your child has been quiet for a short period (a second or two) before you tell her to come out.

Alternatively, if your child is screaming very loudly, simply re-set the timer and tell your child that you have started again.

If your child does not want to leave time-out, that's okay. Your child can stay for as long as she likes.

> One child I was seeing was very quiet when the timer went off after time-out. His mother said he could come out, but there was no response, the door did not open. There was no sound from inside his room. After a while she was surprised to see him playing outside. He had climbed out the window back into freedom.
>
> Another child had a different response. He barricaded the door so that his parents could not get in. Many children refuse to come out of time-out (for a while), but this was a bit more extreme. It was a bit like an inmate refusing to leave prison when his time was up. Fortunately, the parents just ignored it, and after a short while, he dismantled the barricade and came out. If they

had made a fuss and tried to force their way in, he would have
been sure to have fought back and he would have enjoyed the
extra attention.

Step 4: After time-out

If your child was placed in time-out for a red card offence,
after time-out, carry on as normal. Do not lecture, do not
spend a lot of time explaining. Do not give lots of cuddles
straight away. Rather, wait until your child has behaved well
for a few minutes, then give positive attention.

If, however, your child got a warning yellow card, the situation is slightly different. Your child got the yellow card
because she refused to follow an instruction. If you do not
revisit this, she still has got away with not doing as she is told.
So as soon as time-out has ended, you must repeat the instruction and go through the whole process again, until your child
has completed the task.

For this reason, you need a fair bit of time when dealing
with disobedience. If you are in a hurry to get out it is best just

to leave the toys — or whatever — until you get back. Do not start the whole procedure in the first place.

Overcoming time-out problems

Here we will discuss only the two most common time-out problems. The responses to them that are suggested are useful for other time-out problems as well.

Coming out of time-out before the time is up

This is the most common and difficult problem with time-out. There are a number of different solutions. The one you choose will depend on how disruptive your child is, how old your child is, and what you feel most comfortable with.

1 **Increasing the time-out period.** Each time your child comes out of time-out, take her back and say, 'That's an extra minute.' Add an extra minute to the time-out period every time your child comes out. Obviously, this is only suitable for older children (over five years) who have some idea of what 'one minute' is.

2 **Holding.** If you use the bedroom, you can hold the bedroom door handle for the time period. If you use time-out in a chair, you can try to hold your child in the chair. However, this can result in a struggle, so it is best to put her straight into a room where you can close the door.

3 **Removing privileges.** If your child will not stay in time-out, you can remove a privilege instead. You should have a list of at least ten small things you can deprive your child of. These should be important to your child.

Choose privileges from the following list to remove:

- losing a favourite toy for one hour
- missing a favourite television program
- missing evening television
- going without dessert or ice cream
- not going to a friend's house
- removing bicycle for two hours
- taking away pocket money
- no computer for the rest of the day
- no PlayStation, X-Box, Gamecube for the rest of the day
- going to bed half an hour early
- missing out on playing with Mum or Dad.

Remember to fine *one* thing *each* time your child comes out of time-out without permission.

Destroying rooms

If you have put your child in the bedroom, and at the end of time-out you find that your child has made a mess, you can either:

- tell her that she must stay there until it is cleaned up, OR
- re-set the timer and give an extra period of time-out (best for children under five).

Time-out in public places

Children often misbehave when taken out in public — going shopping or visiting friends or relatives, for example. During these times, it is often difficult for parents to control mis-behaviour.

Below are some guidelines that may make it easier for you to take your child out in public. It is important that your child has been disciplined within the home, using the time-out procedure outlined previously, before this is attempted. It is also important to remember that this procedure only works for children aged three years and over.

- At first, make shopping trips as short as possible. This will reduce the chance of your child becoming bored. Try to arrange trips when it is not too hot, and when your child is not too tired or hungry.
- Let your child help with the shopping by giving her things to do. If your child is carrying one fairly heavy item in each hand, she will not be able to run off so easily.
- Explain to your child what you expect of her ('I want you to stay close to me and no tantrums in the shops'). Explain what will happen if your child does not comply and, importantly, what will happen if she does (see below).
- If your child is behaving herself, make sure that you remember to let her know by frequently using the running commentary and labelled praise: 'You are being such a good girl, you are helping mummy carry her shopping.'
- Carry a texta with you. Before shopping or visiting, show the texta to your child. Tell your child that if she throws a tantrum, runs away from you, or does not do as you say, you will put a cross on her hand (or your hand if she is likely to rub it off).

- Explain to your child that each cross will earn her time-out as soon as you get home (up to a maximum of ten minutes for children aged three to six and 20 minutes for older children).

- As soon as your child starts to misbehave, show her the texta and tell her that if she does not do as she is told, he will get a cross. If she continues to misbehave, mark your child's hand with a cross.

- When you get home, point out the cross and say, 'You have a cross — you did not do as you were told and must go to time-out.'

- If, on the other hand, your child behaves during the shopping trip, give her a small reward. This can be stopping at the park on the way home to play, or buying an ice cream.

In a nutshell

- Discipline methods work best if your child is getting as much attention as possible for cooperative behaviour.
- Reasoning, nattering, yelling and smacking all mean your child is getting extra attention for disruptive behaviour.
- Ignoring only works for tantrums and whining. It is not very effective for aggressive behaviour or disobedience. Time-out works best for these.
- Aggressive behaviour and defiance (arguing with the referee) are red card offences and result in immediate time-out with no warnings.
- Disobedience is a yellow card offence. Only one warning yellow card is given. The next time your child is disobedient means a red card. (For disobedience, make sure your child cooperates with your request as soon as time-out is over. If not, repeat the procedure.)

Part 2

The first social skills

So far we have talked about behaviour. This is very important and affects how well a child will cooperate at school and whether or not he will get along with his peers. Other children will not want to play with a child who is always argumentative or aggressive. They will also not be attracted to a child who is passive and unresponsive. Without developing a degree of cooperation, your child will have more difficulty learning other social skills.

In Part 2 we will discuss how parents can influence their child's social skills. We will learn how important basic social skills are in a child's development. The first social skills, such as greeting skills, and taking turns listening, talking and playing, lay the foundations for getting along with others.

While most parents are concerned about their child's academic skills and their abilities in the three Rs, research is showing that social skills may be just as important. A child with good social skills is likely to have fewer problems later with depression, anxiety and other social problems.

Children with good social skills also do better at school. First, teachers and other students like them more. Second, there is a strong link between good social skills and good academic performance. This may be because they are better listeners; they listen to instructions and cooperate more. They also manage emotions and problem solve well. They think about the consequences of their actions, and because of this they are more motivated to learn.

8 How parents can help

I was asked to observe a four-year-old boy, Thomas, at a local preschool. Thomas was a little behind in some areas. He did not seem to be able to grasp some of the more basic skills, such as counting, colours, etc. He was having difficulty with fine motor skills such as holding a pencil. He was also having a lot of trouble socially. I watched him for a couple of hours. Thomas was not cooperative with the teachers, and any request, no matter how simple (even asking him to sit down for a story), was met with screams of protest. Whenever another child approached Thomas he would become upset, thrash his arms about and tell them to go away. He did not do much apart from play with his favourite train. He looked very miserable.

Later, Thomas's mother, Michelle, talked to the early childhood teacher, who was very experienced. They were discussing whether Thomas would be ready for school the following year. Michelle was very concerned and was willing to help in any way she could. I listened as she talked about working on his counting and colours as well as taking him to an occupational therapist to help him with his coordination.

'Then he should be ready for school,' said Michelle.

'That's good, but it's not his colours and numbers I'm most worried about.' said the teacher. 'I'm worried about his social skills. I'm worried about how he's going to get along with the other children.'

Research has identified five main skill areas that are essential for a child if he is going to experience a successful start at school.

Of course if your child is delayed in any of these areas, but is of school age, the school can arrange for extra assistance for your child. This needs to be discussed with the school before you enrol your child. The skill areas that are essential for school success are:

1   **Attitude to learning.** A child's attitude to learning is most affected by (if not dependent on) whether he is cooperative with the teacher or defiant. He must be able to follow instructions, concentrate on what he is doing and ignore distractions. He should be open to learning and have some persistence in new tasks.

2   **Social skills.** A child needs to have reasonable social skills in order to get along with others, both adults and children. He should be able to wait his turn, share, express feelings appropriately and have some control over his emotions.

3   **Physical and independence skills.** A child needs fine and gross motor skills that are good enough for him to manage tasks at school. He should be able to use the toilet and be as independent as possible with dressing. He should also be able to hold a pencil and use scissors.

4   **Language skills.** A child needs to be able to listen, understand what is being said and express himself. An interest in books is also a real plus.

5   **Cognitive development.** A child should have some basic general knowledge and basic knowledge of numbers and letters (be familiar with the ABC, for instance).

The first of these, attitude to learning, is essentially a child's willingness to cooperate. This can be greatly helped by working through Part 1 of this book. Of the remaining skills that are considered necessary for school, social skills are considered by many teachers the next most important, but the most often overlooked.

My son Martin (then five) had just started kindergarten. We thought he was lucky to have a good teacher, Mrs Mac. One day, I picked him up from school and asked him how his day was.

'Oh good. Mrs Mac said I was manure.' There was a hint of pride in the way he said it, but this only made me hesitate a moment before doing a U-turn and heading back to school to find Mrs Mac.

'Martin said you called him manure,' I said.

There was a brief look of concern on Mrs Mac's face as she tried to understand what I was talking about. Then she realised what had happened.

'Oh, I remember. There was an incident and I thought Martin was going to get upset, but he controlled himself and calmed down. I said he was *mature.*'

When my colleagues and I were developing a social skills program for pre-school children, I spent a number of weeks observing children at preschools. I wanted detailed observations of how children interacted with each other. I also wanted to find out how children differed in the way they related to one another. I compared three groups of children.

First, I observed the children the preschool teachers rated as the most popular; these were children most liked by others.

Second, I observed children who were rated by teachers as being antisocial; these were the most difficult and aggressive.

Third, I looked at the children who were the most shy and withdrawn.

Although I observed many children, the examples below are fairly typical of the three different types.

The popular child. Dan was always playing and chatting with the other children. When he wanted to join in he went up to the other children and asked about what they were doing. He smiled a lot, took turns, shared and laughed a lot. The other children liked him.

The antisocial child. Jeremy (aged four) had just entered the sandpit, pushed a girl over and grabbed her spade. He then saw a boy with a bucket, went over and yelled at him very loudly and in a very aggressive manner. Jeremy grabbed the bucket; there was a tussle as the other boy refused to let go. That was until Jeremy whacked the boy with his spade. The boy cried and gave up the bucket. Jeremy was then happy shovelling sand into the bucket. But only for a while ...

The shy child. Isaac was very shy. He just sat on his own. If another child came up to him, he would look away and not respond at all. Most of the day he followed his favourite teacher around and would not leave her side. If she was too busy, Isaac would cry; often he was comforted by another teacher.

The observations revealed a number of skills that the more popular children exhibited, but that the antisocial and shy children lacked:

- **_Greeting skills._** When the more popular children greeted and spoke to others, adults or children, they had good eye contact and looked at the person they were talking to. They smiled a lot — about 60 percent of the time. The shy children did not look at, smile or speak to others much at all. The antisocial children looked down at the ground, as though they were guilty and had done something wrong (which they often had). Often the only time they smiled was when they had just hit someone. The shy, withdrawn children had very little eye contact. (Of course it must be remembered that in some cultures it is a sign of disrespect for a child to look 'an elder' in the eye, so cultural differences must be taken into account for some children.)

  What struck me most about the antisocial and shy children was simply that they did not look very happy. They looked miserable, almost as if they were depressed.

- **_Joining in._** When the popular children joined in with others, they first watched and listened while the other children were playing. They also smiled a lot and asked questions. It was as if they were tuning into the play. The children with more antisocial behaviour usually joined in by pushing someone else out of the way. Their tone of voice was very aggressive and they shouted and did not listen. Although they wanted to play with others and tried to join in a lot, they were often rejected by the other children. The shy children simply did not try to join in. If other children approached them, they either ignored them or became upset.

- *Listening and talking.* The popular children talked and listened. The antisocial children talked but did not listen. The shy children listened but did not talk.

- *Taking turns and sharing.* The popular children also played differently. They took turns at play and shared. They were more likely to reason and put their point of view and also more likely to listen to others' reasoning. The antisocial children did not take turns, they just took. The very shy children simply did not interact very much. Sadly, they were largely ignored by the other children.

How parents can help children with each of these skills will be dealt with in the following chapters.

Many parents feel at a loss about how to help a child learn social skills. After all, most of a child's interactions with other children occur at childcare, preschool or school, when the parent is not around. There are, however, many ways parents can help children learn social skills so that children can be more confident with their peers. Here are ten ways parents can help:

1   **Increasing cooperation and building a positive parent–child relationship.** Parenting skills designed to enhance cooperation were covered in Part 1 of this book, but cannot be emphasised enough. If a child is not cooperative with others and is aggressive and loud, other children will avoid him. Similarly, if a child is stubborn and refuses to interact with others, other children simply will not bother. The best way to improve your child's cooperative behaviour is to go through the steps in Part 1. This will build a more

positive relationship between you and your child. The relationship between you and your child is your child's first and most important relationship. It sets the stage for his other relationships in life.

2   **Setting an example.** It is easy for parents to forget that they are being watched all the time by their child. The child might not look as if he is paying attention, but he sure is listening. Social skills can be taught by example: from how a parent just says a cheery 'Hello' or uses good manners, such as saying 'please' and 'thank you', to how parents resolve conflict in their own relationship or with others. All these are situations that your child will observe. How you behave will influence how he behaves.

3   **Playing with children.** Playing with children can teach important social skills. Studies show that children who are more liked by both other children and teachers are children whose parents play with them using few commands and lots of encouragement. Children whose parents are dictatorial and critical are less liked by other children. Chapter 4 described ways parents can play with children using few directions and more positive attention.

Through play, children also learn to share, take turns, cooperate and negotiate. Different play activities can also encourage the learning of different social skills; these activities will be described in the following chapters.

It is often difficult for parents to find the time to play with their children. Mothers especially are very hard-pressed, and a number of recent studies still show that mothers do significantly more household chores than fathers. Being a modern father, I did not believe any of these studies applied to me. I was different, and the men in those studies were not like me at all. I was brought back to reality fairly abruptly one day when I was playing with my daughter, Nicola, then aged four.

As we were playing, she said: 'It's good that we get Mum to do all the jobs, so we can just play!'

4   **Talking to children about relationships.** Children who have regular conversations with parents about their peer relationships are better liked by other children. It is important to talk to children about relationships — not in an intense way, but as part of normal conversation, such as on the trip to and from school and preschool, at mealtimes etc. Many parents complain that when they ask their children what they did at preschool or school, their child just responds 'Nothing' or 'Not much'.

If this happens, get into the habit of asking specific questions, such as 'What did you do at lunchtime?', 'Who did you play with?' 'Did you have a story today?' 'Did you make something? What was it?' Do not forget to ask who your child played with and what they played and what happened. These should not be interrogations, but conversations to find out ('Oh, and what did you do then?') and to prompt ('Do you think that was a good idea?'). Making a habit of talking to your child about his play with other children also gives your child the opportunity to tell you if he is being teased or bullied.

Talk to your children about friendship. Ask them to think of some words that would describe a good friend. Examples might be: honest, fun, kind, interesting.

5   **Provide children with opportunities to play with other children.** Children who have had opportunities to play with others adapt better to preschool and school. Your child will learn best how to interact with others by playing. Here are a few guidelines to help:

Have children in your home. It is best if your child's first experiences of playing with others happen at home, so you can supervise and provide help and support. It is important to provide some structure, especially at first. Start with refreshments and then go on to toys that might be easy to share, such as a dolls' house, action figures or sand play or playdough. Ball games are also good fun. Do not use toys that your child is possessive about. If he does not want to share them, put them away. Do not use toys that are difficult to share, such as a train set with only one train.

Keep early play experiences small (in numbers) and short (in time). Start by asking only one or two children over. Do not make these sessions too long at first — a hour or two is plenty. You can build up to longer times later.

Supervise. This is the most important thing of all. Do not just leave the children to play by themselves. Do not take over everything, but keep an eye on the children so that you can intervene to help them resolve disputes or distract them onto other activities if things are not going smoothly. As they get older and more confident you can gradually let them play more independently.

6   **Prompt and praise.** The supervision you give young children (under fives) in their play should be mainly positive. Give the children plenty of encouragement for sharing or playing nicely. Prompt the children if they are not playing according to the rules: 'Perhaps Simon would like a turn now.' Do not forget to praise any cooperation.

7   **For young children, consider childcare or preschool.** If your child is of preschool age (ages three to five years), preschools and childcare centres can have a positive effect on social skills. Children who attend preschool or childcare are generally more socially competent than children who do not. The quality of care is important. Preschools with well-trained and experienced staff and which provide structured programs offer a better learning experience. Some centres offer special programs for social skills. Ask the director what the centre does to develop children's social skills.

8   **Extra activities.** In some neighbourhoods there may be no children close by who are a similar age to your children. In this case it is a good idea to seek out other activities where your child learns to interact with other children. These opportunities can be found for younger children (from eighteen months to five years) in playgroups, and other activities such as gym and music classes. For school-aged children, organised sports, girl guides or scouts can all provide supervised opportunities for your child to learn to get along with others.

9   **Learning skills through reading and television.** When you are reading story books to your child you

can comment on the characters' social skills (or in some books, the lack of them) as you are reading. 'Oh, wasn't he polite, saying please and thankyou?' or 'Was that a nice thing to say? How do you think the other child felt?' You can use television in the same way. There are specially written books for children on different social skills (see Further reading).

10 **Make up stories about social situations.** A good way of teaching children how to behave in social situations is to make up a story. This is only limited by your imagination. The story should be about a boy or girl similar in age to your child. It should describe how a child might behave in different situations. An example is given in the next chapter.

Michelle worked very hard with Thomas throughout the year. I spent some time helping her with behaviour management techniques to help Thomas cooperate. Michelle prompted him to greet other people and look at them when he spoke. She played with him every day as often as she could and taught him to take turns and share. She watched his play with others closely and corrected him if be became upset or difficult. Soon Thomas was cooperating much more with teachers and was happy playing with other children. Importantly, Thomas was learning more. Had he continued his defiance with teachers, he would not have learned the cognitive or other skills he needed.

The following chapters discuss in more detail how parents can teach children specific social skills such as greeting, joining in, listening and talking, taking turns and sharing.

Social skills are complex, and some children find them difficult to learn. If you try to teach them all at once, it can be overwhelming for children; it is best to concentrate on one skill at a time. For example, when teaching greeting skills, as described in the next chapter, just focus on this skill for one week. When your child is greeting others nicely, go on to the next skill.

In a nutshell

- Educational experts consider social skills of considerable importance in a child's adjustment to school.
- Popular children smile more and use eye contact when greeting others. They also take turns, share and listen more.
- There are many ways parents can help their child learn social skills. Setting an example, playing games that encourage turn-taking, providing opportunities for mixing with others and just talking about relationships can all help.

Greeting

Social interaction is critical in humans from the first moments of life. The newborn baby is physically helpless. In other species, newborn animals can crawl or walk to find their mother soon after birth. Human babies only have eye contact to help them survive. By gazing into his mother's eyes, the baby is saying, 'Don't leave me, I need you, look after me.' This is the baby's first greeting.

Social interaction remains an important factor throughout a person's life. Few things bring us as much joy as a fulfilling relationship, and yet social relationships are also responsible for our lowest lows. Greetings are the beginning of any social interaction, and are important from birth right throughout our life. Research on marriages show that how couples greet each other or say goodbye is a powerful predictor of whether the couple will separate or stay together. Couples who take time to say hello and show some form of affection when leaving for work or coming home are much more likely to stay together. In other interactions, whether at work or in social situations, greetings are important. People who welcome you with a genuine smile, a hello and a handshake (or a kiss) are much easier to bond with than those who avoid eye contact and mumble a greeting.

Greeting skills are important for children, as a child who responds with a happy smile is likely to be talked to more.

> Sally went into preschool and her teacher said, 'Hello Sally.'
> Sally said, 'Hello Bernadette' and smiled. Bernadette smiled back and said, 'I love your shoes, are they new?' Sally said, 'Yes, I got them yesterday.' Bernadette said, 'Well they're beautiful!'
> Sally went in and started playing. Her friend came in and said, 'Hello.' Sally smiled and said, 'Hello' back. Soon they were playing with each other.

A child who does not respond to others with any form of greeting often puts a stop to further interaction.

> When Jodie's preschool teacher greeted her, Jodie just looked down at the floor and looked very uncomfortable. Jodie's teacher thought she would not press it, because it might embarrass Jodie further, so she just let it go.
> When another girl came up to play with Jodie and said, 'Hello', Jodie just turned her head and ignored her. Soon, the girl got bored and went off to play with someone else. Jodie was left by herself.

Clearly, if Jodie continues to react this way when others greet her, adults and children alike will tend to leave her alone. She will miss out on hundreds of interactions. It is only through these interactions that children learn more complex social skills. Without these social skills, Jodie will find it harder and harder to make friends.

Many children go through a shy phase from around the toddler age. They may go from smiling at everyone to hiding behind Mum if anyone speaks to them. By the time they are three they usually grow out of this. However, some very shy and anxious children do not grow out of it, and become very with- drawn. Also, some children with difficult behaviour — such as diso- bedience and defiance — are also less likely to greet and respond to

Couples who take time to ... show some form of affection ... are much more likely to stay together.

others. These children prefer to look at the ground. If these children can be taught to greet others, it can be the start of changing how others react to them.

There are three main components of greeting skills:

1   eye contact
2   saying hello
3   smiling.

Isabelle was six years old and still very shy. If anyone spoke to her she would focus her gaze on the ground and would not respond at all. Isabelle was being taught a social skills program in her kindergarten class. She had just completed the first session on greeting skills. This session taught children the three skills of eye contact, saying hello and smiling.

It was afternoon, and Isabelle's mum was picking her up from school. As Isabelle was getting into the car her mum said:

'Hello Isabelle, did you have a good day at school?'

Isabelle said: 'Mum, you're supposed to look at me and smile when you're saying hello!'

As explained in Chapter 8, it is best to concentrate on one skill at a time, so over one week, try as many of the following activities as you can. The most important thing to remember is to make it fun.

You are a role model

Remember that you are your child's most important role model. Start with modelling a cheery 'Hello' at home first thing in the morning, when you come home, and when you pick the children up from school or preschool. Use 'prompt and praise' with your child to let her know that you expect a reply. For example:

> 'I just said hello to you, Jane. What do you say?'
> 'Hello, Mum.'
> 'That's a good girl for saying hello with such a nice smile.'

Practise greetings every day as a family, and don't forget to make sure you try to greet others in a friendly way.

> I am not a morning person. I get up, and before I have a cup of tea even a simple task such as finding my slippers seems insurmountable. My cheery wife and even more cheery eight-year-old son always beam happily and say, 'Good morning, Dad!' I am afraid I barely manage eye contact, and my attempt at a smile is pathetic. However, I do summon up my last resources and mumble 'Lo.' My 14-year-old daughter has inherited my morning genes, but we persevere with her and try to prompt and praise:
>
> > 'Nicola, Martin said, "Good morning."'
> > Nicola: 'Grn.'
> > 'You're a good girl for grunting.'

Puppets and dolls

Young children (up to five) who are very shy and not very talkative with others are often more comfortable using puppets or dolls to talk. Most young children love playing with puppets, and parents can use puppets to engage children in social interaction. Playing with puppets with your child presents lots of opportunities to say hello. You can make other comments, such as, 'Oh, Bertie (the puppet) looked at me when he said hello and gave me a lovely smile.'

Playing with dolls or dolls' houses or action figures also gives opportunities for lots of hellos, goodbyes, good lucks and see you laters.

Dramatic play

Playing shops or games with a similar theme provides lots of opportunities for children to greet others. You can set up a shop with items displayed with prices. You may have a drawer for money or a cash register. Children usually enjoy being the shopkeeper, which means they need to greet you and say hello. You may reply that you were so pleased they said hello in such a cheery way and point out that they looked at you and smiled.

A post office stocked with paper, envelopes, pens, stamps, stamp pads, stapler, scales and a mailbox made out of cardboard also serves the same function.

Another variation on this theme is to play doctors or hospitals. A doctor kit, bandages and sticky plasters can be used. (Many doctors do not have the best social skills and some universities recognise this and have special courses to teach trainee doctors how to communicate and empathise with their patients. This shows how important social skills are in all areas of life.)

You could also set up a garage where bikes can be taken for repair. A few tools, pretend petrol pump, torch and a bit of oil will do.

Playing restaurants is fun, too. You can set up a small table with a tablecloth, plates and cutlery, plus a kitchen area, a drawer or cash register for money and a few 'credit cards'. Your child can be the waiter, and can greet and serve you and answer questions. She might also have to deal with some complaints.

Talk with your child about good manners, and about saying hello and goodbye

Talk with your child about good manners. Remind her that if someone speaks to her it is polite to answer. Let her know that she should look at others when saying hello and goodbye. You might talk to your child about greeting others when you are expecting visitors, on the way to a friend's house or to the local shop. You might say, 'Matthew and his mum are coming in a few minutes. When they knock, let's go to the door and say hello.' When the time comes, do not forget to model a good example of greeting and to praise your child for any attempt.

When watching television, you can comment on the manners of the children in the program: 'Look at the way she looked and smiled when she said hello; that was good manners', or, 'That boy was rude. He ignored it when the man said hello.' Also, point out other manners, such as saying please and thank you.

You can also comment on manners when reading books, and there are books that talk about greeting skills — *Hello! How are you?* by Shigeo Watanabe, for example (see Further reading).

Other activities

Teach your child some songs. Here are a few suggestions:

- 'Two fat gentlemen meet in a lane. How do you do? (or Hello to you).'
- 'Hello, hello, hello and how are you today? I'm fine, I'm fine and I hope that you are too.'

Also, try teaching your child to say hello or goodbye in different languages: bonjour, ciao, bon giorno or hola. It might be fun to make up a greetings from around the world poster. Find a map of the world and put stickers on the different countries with 'Hello' written in the language of each country.

My colleagues and I recently published a study that showed that a group of preschool children with social difficulties could be taught social skills using small groups. In the groups, children were taught social skills using puppets, stories, songs, videos and activities.

At the end of the PALS program, which went for ten weeks, the children were observed and rated by the teachers. It was found that the children's social skills — greeting, eye contact, listening, taking turns and sharing — all had improved. What was also encouraging was that children who had shown aggressive behaviour were less aggressive after the group. They had learned alternative ways of behaving. The shy children were also much more confident, and responded to others.

The best thing about it was that the children enjoyed it and found it fun. Children not included in the group kept asking if they could join in, so we did it for the whole class. Better still, many parents remarked on how their shy children had grown in confidence and were much better equipped to start school.

This is different from the late 1960s and early 1970s, when aversion therapy was very popular. This was most famously depicted in the film, *A Clockwork Orange*, directed by Stanley Kubrick, where Alex, a violent youth, was 'treated' by being shown videos of fights while simultaneously having electric shocks administered. Alex became conditioned against fighting. Some Californian psychologists used aversion therapy on severely autistic children to teach them to 'socialise' with adults. Fortunately, these methods were widely condemned and are no longer in use.

My only close-up experience with aversion therapy was when I was a clinical psychology student doing an internship at a psychiatric hospital. My supervisor was very keen on aversion therapy and asked me to sit in while she was 'treating' a young man who had been referred because he was cross-dressing. The man was asked to bring in some of his favourite dresses, and was wired up to the 'shock-box'. I sat opposite him.

As the man held a dress, my supervisor gave him an electric shock. It was a big one, as the man leapt out of his seat and flew across to where I was sitting and grabbed hold of me. Which meant that I was being shocked too. I don't think this supervisor liked me very much, because she took an awfully long time to turn off the electricity. We seemed to dance around for an age, jerking fitfully, and he wouldn't let go. It put me off dresses for life.

Joining in

It is a fact of life in preschools that one-half of all attempts by children to join in with others' play are rejected. So teaching children to join in has a 50–50 chance of failure. This makes joining in a difficult skill to teach. When my daughter first went to preschool I wanted to stay with her the whole day, just to make sure the other children were nice to her. Unfortunately, children have to learn to take the knocks.

Some children are too shy and fearful to approach a group of other children or initiate a conversation. These children are often neglected by the others. Other children are the opposite extreme. They are too enthusiastic and eager to join in. They impulsively charge into another group of children without waiting to be accepted or learning the rules of the game. They often push others out of the way and try to take over. After a while these children are often rejected by others.

There are three basic skills that can help children learn to join in:

1   **Watch.** Children often just spend some time on the edge of the group, watching what the other children are doing. This can help your child tune in to the game and its rules. It also gives your child time to decide if she really wants to join in with that group. Does she want to play that game? Are the other children too boisterous and wild?

2   **Compliment.** Not many people, including children, can resist flattery. If children say things like: 'This looks like a fun game!' or 'You're really clever with those blocks, it looks great!' or 'That was a great goal', it is harder to reject them.

3   **Questions.** If a child just watches and asks questions about the game, this can help. Making a suggestion about what she can do in the game can also be useful: 'I could drive the blocks over to you in the truck', for instance. Or she could just say, 'This looks like a great game — can I play?'

One way of explaining these skills to children is to make up a story. The idea is to make a story with a name similar to your child's (Mick instead of Nick, or Sally instead of Sarah, for example). The age of the child should be the same age as your child. This helps your child identify more with the story. A joining in story might go something like this:

Sally was four years old. She was playing by herself one day at preschool. She saw a group of children playing in the block corner. She went over to the corner and watched for a little while. The other children were quite boisterous and were knocking over each other's buildings, and one boy threw a block at another girl. Sally decided she did not want to play there.

Sally then went over to the dress-up corner. A group of children were playing with the different costumes. They were pretending to be characters from a children's television series.

Sally said, 'That looks like fun!'

'Yes,' said the others.

'Can I be the witch?' Sally said.

'No, we're not having witches in this game.'

Sally felt a bit upset, and she walked away. Then she noticed another group of children in Home corner. She went over and watched. One boy was playing daddy and he was cooking with his children.

'You make a great daddy and children. It's funny,' said Sally.

'Thanks,' said 'daddy'.

'Do you want a mummy?' said Sally.

'Yes please,' said the children.

They all had a great game together.

Stories like this can be very helpful for teaching children the steps to take in social situations. The story above teaches the three steps: watching, complimenting and joining in. It also teaches that rejection is likely to happen at some time, and to try again if this happens. With 50 percent of all attempts at joining in being met with rejection, it is important to prepare your child for the possibility of rejection. For further information about making up stories to help children in a variety of situations Doris Brett's *Annie Stories* is a useful book (see Further reading).

Another way of helping children to join in is for you to demonstrate when your child is playing. If your child is playing happily with her dolls' house, go up and sit close by and watch. Then compliment her in some way: 'I love the way you've tidied up the dolls' house. It looks great, and you're having such a fun game.' Then ask if you can join in: 'Shall I be grandma?'

It is best to prompt your child to join in — at first — when she is likely to be most successful. For example, when you visit friends or relatives, the other children are familiar and are less likely to be rejecting. You might say, 'Remember what happened in the story? Sally just watched for a while, then said something nice to the other children before she asked to join in.'

In a nutshell

- Greeting skills are the start of any social interaction. Without them, no further interaction occurs.
- There are three important things to learn when greeting others: eye contact, saying hello and smiling.
- Practise new skills at home first: model greeting others and prompt and praise your children for greeting others.
- Set up activities such as playing shops and post offices to practise greeting skills.
- Teach your child to watch others and compliment them before trying to join in with their game.
- Comment on how other children use good social skills in books and on television.
- Make up stories or find books on different skills.

Listening and talking

'He just won't listen.'

'She just doesn't take any notice of me.'

'I have to ask him to do something ten times before he does it.'

'I ask him what I just said and he gives me a blank look.'

These are the most common complaints I hear from parents about their children. Many children just switch off when they are being spoken to. Yet listening is a very important social skill. Conversation consists of learning to listen and to talk in turn.

Children need to listen when they are in preschool or the classroom. If they do not listen, they will not learn. They have to listen to instructions so they know what to do.

I was running a social skills group for children in a local preschool. One child would not listen at all; he kept pushing, poking and annoying the other children. He talked while others were speaking and tried to get attention the whole time. I sat him away from the others but he crawled under a table and made loud noises. He then climbed up onto the table and did a dance and barked like a dog. It was impossible to continue. I could not get through the session, and it was obvious that none of the other children had learned anything as they were too distracted.

A survey found that 35 percent of teachers said that they lost between two and four hours' teaching time a week because of children who would not listen. A disruptive student not only fails to listen and learn; he affects other students too. The academic performance of the child sitting next to a disruptive student can drop by as much as 30 percent because he is distracted so much.

Many children with disruptive behaviour have problems with listening and understanding what is being said. In class these children quickly lose track of the information that is being given by the teacher. They give up and act the clown instead.

In my work I give a lot of lectures and workshops. Most lecturers will tell you that there is nothing more distracting than someone who talks to her neighbour, giggles and yawns. On the other hand, there is nothing more gratifying than having someone who is sitting and looking straight at you, except when she is scribbling away frantically trying to jot down your words of wisdom. The person nods a lot, smiles, and laughs at your jokes. I remember giving a lecture at a national conference of psychologists. I was talking about the social skills program we had developed. There was one person in the audience who was particularly attentive, and who was nodding and looking and smiling. At the end of my talk, when it was question time, she put her hand up and said, 'It's not really a question, but I just wanted to tell you that they used your program at my daughter's preschool and it was fantastic. It has made her so much more confident.' I would have happily paid her to say that.

When I was a university student we used the power of attentive listening to change our lecturer's behaviour. When a lecturer stood on the right side of the lecture room we would all look bored, cough, yawn, scrape our chairs, look out the window and make distracting noises.

When he stood on the left side, we all looked up attentively, nodded wisely, took notes, laughed at his jokes and asked intelligent questions.

By the end of the talk, the lecturer was glued to the left-hand side of the room. We had modified his behaviour without his knowing by using our listening skills. Such is the power of attentive listening.

There are two main components to listening skills:

1   Make eye contact (which children have been practising for their greeting skills — see Chapter 9)
2   Do not talk while someone else is talking.

This can be summed up as 'Look, shh and listen.' Here are some ways to help improve listening skills in children.

For young children (three to five years)

- **Play talking on the telephone.** Let your child call you using a toy telephone, or pretend with a mobile phone. On the telephone, only one person can talk at a time, so this will help your child learn to take turns.

    You can also make a talking telephone by using a few metres of plastic tubing and two funnels. Push a funnel into each end of the tube. You can then take turns talking down the funnel and listening.

    Alternatively, you can use two tin cans (make sure there are no sharp edges) and a length of string. Make a hole in the middle of the closed end of each can. Thread the string through and tie a knot. Join it to the other can (so that the cans are back to back, so to speak) and repeat. If you pull the string tight you should be able to hear each other when you talk into the can from a distance.

- **Play 'mystery sounds'.** Ask your child(ren) to close their eyes and try to recognise different sounds. While their eyes are closed, make different noises. It may be a whistle, the microwave, a spoon and cup, a handclap, keys jangling.
- **Tap a rhythm.** While their eyes are closed, tap out a rhythm on a table. Ask the children to tap out the same rhythm. Gradually make it harder.

For all children

- **Mealtimes.** Mealtimes can be a good time to practise taking turns listening and talking. Take it in turns to talk about what happened in your day. If your child interrupts while you are talking, you might say, 'Just a minute, let me finish first.' You may need to use a visual signal such as gently holding your hand up. When you have finished, give your child a cue that it is his turn. It is a good idea to finish what you say by asking a question: 'And what did you do at school today, Jack?'

- **Talk to your child.** Research shows that parents who talk to and read to their children more have children with better language skills. On the other hand, parents who are depressed are often too tired and preoccupied to talk to their children as much. Understanding speech is quite complex: it involves attending, learning to process sounds, and then making sense of those sounds. Children need practice at listening and decoding the sounds. Parents can give children this practice by talking to them:
  - Tell your child about your day or things that happened in your childhood.
  - In Chapter 4 we discussed the use of the running commentary when playing with your child. Use this during the day. Also use the running commentary to describe your own behaviour. For example, if you are putting together your child's toy you might say, 'Now I need to find the piece that goes here. Here it is, and now this piece goes on top of it.' Your child might not look as though he is paying attention, but if you talk to him he will take it in.
- **Read to your child.** Reading to children can start at a very early age, and can be continued for most of primary school. You might ask some questions about the story. For example, you might say, 'So what did the boy do that made his brother so angry?' Or 'What do you think will happen next?' This will let you know if your

child is paying attention to the story, and will help him listen for meaning.

- **Use CDs or audiotapes.** Providing children with personal CD or audiotape players can go a long way towards preventing boredom on those long car trips (especially after the 30th game of 'I Spy'). Tapes or CDs of stories work well. These can be great for fostering listening skills in children. It captures their attention and helps with listening and understanding speech. Some music CDs can be good too.

- **Give clear and simple instructions.** This was dealt with in Chapter 5, and is very important in helping your child develop good listening skills. If your instructions go on and on, your child will simply turn off. If you use instructions that are clear and concise, your child is more likely to pay attention.

- **Prompt and praise.** This is an important practice for teaching all social skills. Prompt your child to listen: 'Now please listen to me.' Ask him to repeat what you have said. Do not forget to praise him if he gets it right.

Does your child have a hearing problem?

If you are concerned about your child's hearing, get it checked. Some tell-tale signs of hearing problems are if your child talks very loudly or if he turns the television up loudly and sits very close to it. Our poor dog is ageing, and is now quite deaf. Because he cannot hear himself very well, he thinks we cannot hear him either, and he barks ridiculously loudly, often in my ear when I am sitting watching the football. The trouble is, he is so deaf he cannot hear me tell him to be quiet.

I was seeing a three-year-old boy, Mark, who was referred to me because of his aggressive behaviour at preschool. He had previously been 'encouraged' to leave other centres because of his biting. The preschool was concerned about his behaviour: he would not do as he was told, made silly noises in story time and would lash out at others in frustration.

As I was taking some background information, Mark's mother reported that Mark had a history of ear infections and had been slow to talk. When watching television he had the volume up very loud and sat right in front of it. I referred Mark for a hearing assessment, and it turned out that he had a significant hearing loss, which fortunately could be treated. As his hearing improved, so did his behaviour.

Apart from a hearing loss, if your child genuinely does not seem to understand what you say, it could be that he has difficulties with comprehension and an assessment by a qualified speech pathologist is advisable. Speech pathologists help children who have difficulties with speaking — such as stuttering and pronunciation (expressive language) — and children who have difficulties with understanding what others are saying (receptive language).

Listening to your child

Conversation is two-way. In a balanced conversation people take turns talking and listening. It is also important that you use good active listening skills yourself: this will encourage your child to talk. Active listening is when you *actively* show your child that you are listening. There are various ways you can do this:

- **Look at your child when your child is speaking.** There is nothing more off-putting to a speaker than if the listener is distracted and looking at something else. If you cannot pay attention to your child at the time, ask him to wait a little while until you can give him your full attention.
- **Use gestures to show you are listening.** Smile, nod your head and use encouraging words such as, 'Really?' 'Fantastic!'
- **Ask 'follow on' questions.** These are questions designed to help your child elaborate on what he is saying.

'What happened then?

'What did the teacher say?'

'How did you do that?

- **Summarise.** When your child has finished, briefly sum up what he has just told you. 'So you learned a lot about volcanoes at school today. I'm glad you are going to do a project on them.' This lets your child know that you have been paying attention to what he has been saying.

In a nutshell

- Encourage your child to take turns talking and listening by encouraging conversation. Tell each other about things that have happened in the day.
- Play listening games such a 'telephones' and mystery sounds.
- Talk to your child, read to your child and play CDs and story tapes.
- Give clear, concise instructions.
- Practise good listening skills yourself with your child. Look at him, nod, smile, ask questions and summarise what he says.
- Arrange a hearing test (through your doctor) if you are concerned about your child's hearing.

Taking turns
and sharing

'I wanted to play with that!' ('That' being whatever her brother happens to be playing with)

'He's got more than me!'

'It's not fair. I won — she cheated!'

Our Western society emphasises individual rights, achievements and competition. The media give us messages that it is good to win and be the best and have the latest gadgets. Also, in our society, the trend is for families to be more insular. There are many houses with home entertainment systems, well-equipped play areas and pools, so many families do not go out to the local facilities and share with others. Children are more isolated and in smaller families than before. They are surrounded by toys that are **just for them.**

Competition and possession must be balanced by cooperating, sharing, and recognising that no one person is more important than any other person: we need to teach our children that turn-taking and sharing are important in our society, so that we counteract the pressure to focus on possessions, winning and being the best.

> Our daughter, Nicola, was counting out her money and was disappointed because she did not have quite enough to get what she wanted. Martin, then aged six, ran into his room and came out with his wallet and counted out the required money, which he gave to her. We were quite stunned (sibling rivalry is usually alive and well in our family).
>
> 'That's very good of you, but you didn't have to do that,' I said.
>
> 'Nah, that's all right. I'll just get some more from that little basket in your room' (where we keep all our loose change).

As with most things, the best place to start teaching children to share and take turns is at home. Children can be encouraged to take turns and share from an early age, but remember, children's capacity for sharing increases with age (see box below).

Children go through stages in the way they play.

Parallel play. Very young children (younger than two) engage in mainly solitary activities, though they watch other children closely. By the end of the second year, children engage in parallel play. They work next to each other, not really interacting, but doing similar things. For example, they may play in the sandpit. One may dig a hole, one may shovel sand through a sand wheel and another may build a mountain.

Associative play. By the ages of three or four, children play together more. It's not always helping each other, but more doing the same thing as each other. For example, *all* the children might dig different holes. At this age they can be encouraged to share and take turns.

Cooperative play. By the age of five, children cooperate with one another on an activity. They might each have different roles: for example, some might build a big sand mountain and others will tunnel through. Children start to modify their ideas in response to other ideas. At this stage, conflict resolution skills emerge more. As children need to coordinate their activities with one another, they need to take others into account as well as express their own ideas. When the ideas differ, they need to learn to resolve the differences.

Here are some activities that can help children learn to share and take turns:

- **Work on cooperative activities.** Work together on a mural, building a pond, digging a garden or planting plants. Working together towards the same goal builds feelings of belonging and teamwork.

   Some activities allow children to engage in much more complex social behaviour than this. Sand play, water play, clay and woodwork, for example, can be used to foster creativity and social interaction that is less structured.

- **Board games encourage children to take turns and wait for their 'go'.** They have to wait, then throw the dice and make their move. These games provide structure for taking turns. Card games such as Uno and Snap are similar.

- **Some sports encourage taking turns more than others.** In cricket, T-ball and baseball, you have to wait your turn to bat and bowl. In tennis, table tennis and volleyball, children must take turns to serve; playing doubles encourages teamwork. Games like boules, bocce and darts (use magnetic darts) also require turn-taking.

- **Encourage children to initiate sharing and taking turns.** For example, it is often tempting to step in and solve a problem by saying, 'Georgia, give Anna some of your paper — she has run out.' Instead, it might be a good idea to say, 'Anna, ask Georgia if you can have some of her paper.'

- **Prompt children to share.** If you have noticed that a child is just finishing with a toy, you might ask her to offer it to another child. You could consider using a timer. When one child's time is up, encourage her to say 'It's your turn now.' Do not forget to praise her for this.

- **Remember that new toys cause a lot more possessiveness.** Give children the choice as to whether or not they want to share a new toy with other children. If you know they will be possessive about it, put it away before other children arrive.

- **Be a good role model for sharing.** When playing something or doing activities with children, share things with them. Ask them to share with you: for example, 'Can I borrow your blue pencil?' Always remember to praise children for sharing.

- **Help children learn to trade.** Divide up a packet of textas or crayons among the children. Tell them to make a picture with lots and lots of colours. This will encourage them to trade one of their colours for a colour another child has.

- **Encourage helping activities.** Encourage children to do jobs that involve looking after things, such as watering plants and feeding animals. Caring for things makes us feel better about ourselves.

- **Tell tales.** This is good fun for the whole family and can be a good exercise for the car. The rules are simple. The first person starts to make up a story 'Once upon a time …' The person can only use one sentence, or else can only speak for a certain time, such as half a minute. When the person stops, the next person must start off where the previous one left off and continue the story. Keep going until a story is finished: '… and they all lived happily ever after.' This exercise is good because it involves taking turns and it helps develop listening skills. The children must listen to what has been said before they continue.

  Another good game for the car that encourages turn-taking is the old faithful 'I Spy'. For younger children (under five), rather than 'I spy with my little eye something beginning with …', you can say 'I spy with my little eye something the colour of …'

We played *a lot* of 'I Spy' in the car on long journeys. As it was often through featureless country where the only objects were sky, grass and trees, it became fairly challenging. Our children came up with some fairly challenging 'I Spys' themselves.

Nicola (then aged five and a half): 'I spy with my little eye something beginning with W.'

Me (after many attempts, all of which I was gleefully told were hopelessly wrong): 'I give in.'

Nicola: 'Wabbit.'

Later …

Nicola: 'I spy with my little eye something beginning with Y.'

Me (after another series of failures): 'I give in.'

Nicola: 'Ute.'

We also played 'I Spy' when Martin was little, and made it easier by using the beginning sounds of words rather than just the letter.

Martin (then five): 'I spy with my little eye something beginning with prick ...'

Me (with rising alarm, wondering where this was going): 'I give in.'

Martin (pointing to the long grass and prickles by the side of the road): 'Prickles.'

In a nutshell

- Encourage your child to take turns by modelling, and by doing a range of activities that involve turn-taking and sharing.
- Plan some activities that involve collaboration, such as murals, posters, greeting cards, garden projects or woodwork.
- Plan some turn-taking activities such as board games, card games, cricket, baseball, boules and darts.

Part 3

Teaching your child important life skills

Controlling our emotions is one of the most difficult things to learn. Some people have trouble controlling emotions throughout their lives. People who cannot control their anger get into frequent conflicts that cause unpleasantness at least and criminal prosecution at worst. Others cannot control fear or anxiety and live a life of worry. The best ages to teach self-control skills are in the years between three and seven. This is when the brain connections which put the brake on the emotional period of the terrible twos (see the Appendix) are laid down. Of course we continue learning through the rest of our lives, but if we can teach children the basics in the early years we are giving them a good start.

The first step towards controlling our emotions is to recognise our own feelings. Many children (and many adults) find it difficult to recognise that they are becoming emotional until it is too late. By then the emotion has welled up and is out of control. Once this has happened, it is difficult to rein it back. Once children learn to recognise emotions early, they can be taught different ways of reacting. They can learn relaxation as a way of curbing the extremes of destructive feelings. They can learn breathing control methods and methods such as 'self-talk', which is a way of talking oneself out of destructive emotions.

All these techniques are presented in the following chapters, and all have been found to be helpful with many children. Some children are not ready to learn all the methods, so it is important not to push it on them. Try again later, and they may be more receptive.

 **Feelings**

Our body is hard-wired to respond to threat or danger. This is called the fight and flight reaction, or the stress response. The liver secretes glucose to give us an instant burst of energy. Adrenaline is released to stimulate the body: to speed up the heart and breathing so that the glucose is quickly transported to the areas that most need it. Our pain threshold also increases.

Stress also induces a queasy feeling in the stomach and an urge to urinate. It is thought that the reason for this is so that the body can easily shed weight so that we can run faster (the flight reaction). When a grizzly bear is chasing you in the wild, a few seconds could mean the difference between life and death.

Of course in our modern times, the most common source of threat is an argument with the neighbours, a call centre operator, the boss, or colleagues. In these situations, tensing up your muscles, hyperventilating, having palpitations and losing control of your bowels and bladder are probably not the most impressive ways of responding.

I was running a social skills program for a particularly challenging group of six-year-olds. We were talking about feelings. I thought I was on safe ground when I started to talk about happy feelings. I asked the children to remember anything that had made them happy. A hand shot up. 'Me, me, me, me!' said Duncan.

'Duncan, can you tell us something that has made you happy?' I said.

'Yeah, my mum, she was really bad. She left Dad. She took drugs. On Saturday night at midnight, Dad came in through my bedroom window and took me away. That made me happy.'

'Oh ... umm ... thank you for that, Duncan.' I was not sure what else to say, so I quickly moved on to the girl sitting next to him, who had her arm in plaster. It was time to move on to other emotions.

'Shirley, can you tell us any times you have been sad?' I said.

'Yeah. I've got a new "uncle" who has come to live with us. He pushed me down the stairs and broke my arm. That made me sad.' There was a pause, and then a look of horror spread across her face. 'Oops, I wasn't supposed to tell anyone that!'

I had a busy time reporting to the child protection services that day.

While there are many emotions, the most basic ones are mad, sad, glad, fear, surprise and disgust. Teaching children to recognise emotions is very important:

- Recognition is the first step to controlling emotions. I had a child in counselling who had severe anger problems. He had done things such as kick a teacher's car, scratch it with a coin, lock himself in a classroom and throw chairs around. We were discussing some of these incidents (which he was not keen to admit) when he pulled his jumper over his face. He then got up and kicked the glass book cabinet. When I pointed out that he might be getting angry he shouted, 'I'm not angry!' If children can learn to recognise early stages of anger they have a better chance of controlling it. Otherwise the anger takes over and is very difficult to control. People who are very quick to anger over little things and who have trouble calming down get into destructive behaviour patterns. These people have more psychological disorders, not to mention physical health problems (see box below).

Many parents talk to their children about the importance of healthy eating and exercise because they want their children to be fit and well. Far fewer parents talk to their children about emotions. Yet being emotionally healthy is very strongly linked to being physically healthy.

One third of all heart attacks occur in people who are NOT overweight and who do not have high levels of cholesterol. Recent studies show that men and women who are prone to anger are three times more likely to have a heart attack than those who are not.

Anger seems more damaging to a person's cardiac system if the person has been angry from a young age. In the 1950s, researchers at the Johns Hopkins School of Medicine gave questionnaires to young men on how they dealt with stress. They have been following up these men to the present day, looking at their cardiac health. This study of 1000 men showed that those who responded to stress with high levels of anger when younger were five or six times more likely to develop heart attacks before the age of 55.

Those who reported high levels of anger when young were up to three times more likely to have other cardiac problems, such as angina, hardening of the arteries, high blood pressure, congestive heart failure and sudden death from heart disease.

With childhood obesity on the rise and the ever-increasing stress in our lives, it is possible that our children will not enjoy as long a life expectancy as we do. There is a danger that they may suffer more chronic diseases — due to lifestyle factors.

Healthy eating, regular exercise and teaching children to manage anger are all things parents can help their children with from an early age.

- As well as recognising their own emotions, children also need to learn to recognise emotions in others. Some children do not learn this very easily. Children with very aggressive tendencies consistently underestimate the fear they see on the faces of other children. They do not realise how scared they make others feel. If these children learn to recognise emotions in others they will be less likely to fight and more likely to work things out in other ways.

Some children have to learn to deal with emotions that they should never have to.

Billy was seven and was a pleasant and polite young boy. His mother said that mostly he was well behaved and he was not disobedient. His teachers reported that he was well behaved in class and was rarely a problem. It was just that he lit fires. He lit fires mainly at home, and set his bedroom on fire. He once lit a fire at school. Then he lit a fire under the cot of his twelve-month-old sister. We started to think that we had a very dangerous delinquent on our hands. Nothing seemed to work and Billy would not say why he did it. We found out one day, though: Billy's mother, a very attractive young woman, arrived looking very battered. Her partner had beaten her severely. The partner had been repeatedly violent, but Billy was too afraid to tell anyone. So he sent up smoke signals instead.

Teaching children to recognise emotions

My son Martin (then seven) was not at all happy about going back to school after two weeks' holiday.

'I don't want to go to school!' he said angrily.

I gave the predictable parent response: 'I know how you feel; I don't want to go to work either.'

'It's all right for you,' came the even angrier response, 'you haven't had two weeks' holiday!'

How can parents teach children to recognise emotions — their own as well as those of others? Several ways are outlined below. One thing to remember, though, is not to only focus on negative emotions. In our society we focus too much on depression and anxiety, and not enough on positive emotions such as happiness, contentment and pride in achievement. If you only give attention to your child when he is sad or angry, it might well reinforce those feelings.

Children with very aggressive tendencies consistently underestimate the fear they see on the faces of other children. They do not realise how scared they make others feel.

- **Point out your child's emotions.** You might start by noticing the basic emotions — happy, sad, angry (glad, sad, mad). Tell your child whenever you notice a particular emotion: 'You look happy today.' Then you might notice more subtle emotions, such as pride: 'You look very pleased with yourself.'

- **Try to get your child to connect his feelings with the situation that produced them.** 'What are you looking so happy about?' 'I've got a surprise for Daddy!'
- **Prompt your child to label his own emotions.** 'You had a good time at the party — how do you feel?', or, 'Oh, your dolly's broken — how did that make you feel?'
- **Let your child know your feelings.** This will help your child learn to connect other people's feelings to their body language and facial expressions. Make sure you do not just focus on negative emotions. Say things like: 'I'm so happy you got a good school report', or, 'It's such a beautiful day — it always makes me feel good when the weather is like this', or, 'I just broke my favourite cup and I feel a bit sad.'
- **Remember, you are a role model.** When expressing angry feelings, it is important to remember that you are acting as a model for your child. If someone is rude to you and you tell your child that it makes you angry, for instance, that's fine. However, if you then go up and punch the person or give him a mouthful of abuse, you are not modelling or responding to that anger in the best way.
- **Point out emotions in other people.** This might be on the television, in a book or in real life. It is a good idea to use picture books and ask your child to name the emotions expressed in the pictures. If there are no

pictures in the story, but there are descriptions of different emotions, show your child the facial expressions that might go with them. Or ask your child to show you or draw a picture of the facial expressions. There are also books available that talk about emotions (see Further reading).

Most children at some stage experience the death of a pet, and this usually provokes very deep feelings of grief and sadness. This can be a good time to talk about emotions.

My daughter, Nicola, was very attached to our beautiful dog Heidi. They were inseparable. They played together most of the day and Heidi would follow Nicola everywhere.

Heidi became very sick with cancer. She was very ill on Nicola's third birthday but looked on and smiled at the party. The next day she died. I have always thought that she knew that it was Nicola's birthday and held on through that day because she did not want to spoil Nicola's special day.

A few days after Heidi died, Nicola and I went for a walk.

'I wonder what Heidi's doing in heaven,' said Nicola.

'I'm not sure; maybe playing ball,' I said.

'Maybe she's going for a walk with Jesus,' said Nicola.

What a beautiful thought.

In a nutshell

- Destructive emotions such as anger are damaging to both psychological and physical health.
- The first step in teaching children to control negative emotions is to help them recognise their emotions.
- Help children recognise their own emotions by pointing out when they look happy etc. It is important to label positive emotions as well as negative.
- Teach your children to recognise other people's emotions by labelling your own emotions and pointing out others' emotions in pictures or on television.

13 Recognising the feelings of others

I was driving behind another car and becoming increasingly frustrated. The car kept slowing down then speeding up, and more than a few times it veered toward the side of the road. My annoyance was growing. Then my wife made one of her insightful comments about the driver.

'She keeps looking back to the back seat. I think she might have a baby capsule there. The baby's probably screaming.'

I noticed that the woman did indeed keep looking back, and appeared to be talking to the middle back seat. My wife was probably right, as usual. My anger immediately dissipated and I dropped right back to give the car more space.

I had been focusing only on what the car had been doing and how it had affected *me*. My wife focused on the other person's perspective and why she might be behaving in that way. How we view a situation can have an enormous effect on the emotions we feel and how we respond to the situation. In the example above, the new perspective transformed my feelings instantly. Feelings of anger and acts of aggression are often a result of misunderstanding. We know that children who are very aggressive often completely misjudge other people's intentions. For example, a child might accidentally bump into an angry child. The angry child will interpret this as being deliberate and might push back or hit.

Joe Simpson, in *Storms of Silence* (Jonathon Cape), ponders why people are so violent towards one another:

> I have always been useless at fighting. The few times when I have attempted to hit an assailant the result has been fairly ineffectual. Either I miss completely or I hit the other man in the wrong place, and so make him hopping mad. I once tried to knee a man in the groin as hard as I could but only caught his inner thigh, and after that things got very bad. On another occasion a drunk headbutted me in a Sheffield nightclub and then collapsed on the floor at my feet with tears streaming down his face. Being smaller than him had meant that he had simply smashed his nose into the top of my head. I never knew why he had decided to hit me in the first place. I had not set eyes on him before.
>
> *(Reprinted by permission of the Random House Group Ltd)*

Children, especially boys, become involved in aggression in a variety of ways — as the aggressor, as the victim, or as the bystander. Interestingly, victims of aggression often have problems with anger control. Bullies do not pick on every child in the school; they choose their victim carefully. The victim must not be as good at fighting as they are, but must give some sort of reaction that will satisfy the bully. A child who just ignores the bully and walks away is not as much fun as a child who reacts to taunts by losing her temper, getting upset and lashing out ineffectually.

Teaching children to consider the feelings of others while not dampening their competitive spirit is a balancing act.

Daniel Goleman, author of *Emotional Intelligence*, blames many of our society's tragedies on a lack of emotional intelligence. Emotional intelligence includes the skills of recognising and understanding our own emotions and the emotions of others. It also involves controlling our emotions. Goleman claims that incidents such as the Columbine massacre (where a student took a gun to school and shot fellow students), and elderly defenceless people being robbed, beaten and even raped, would not exist if everyone were taught to be more emotionally intelligent. We would have more control of our emotions and show more empathy (the capacity to share an emotion with another) towards others.

Yet our society emphasises the importance of competition, winning and individual acquisition, none of which involves considering the feelings of others. Does teaching children to recognise and respect the feelings of others reduce their chances of doing well in a competitive world?

I remember having an interesting conversation with a father who was a nightclub bouncer. His son, Andrew, was referred to me by the school because he was always in fights in the playground. Andrew was only seven years old, but was physically tall and strong. Also, he had been doing karate since he was four. I tried to talk to his dad about discouraging aggression. Andrew's father had a very reasonable argument against this, which went something like:

'Well look, he's no Einstein. He'll never get to university and work in an office like you. We live in a poor area and it's rough. The other kids are rough. When he's older he'll go to rough pubs. He'll meet trouble without a doubt. And what's he going to do for work? He might have to get a job as a bouncer like me. He needs to be tough and to know how to fight.'

We talked for a long time, and in the end we both agreed
that his son did need to be able to fight to defend himself. He
also needed to learn not to deliberately provoke others and go
looking for trouble. We parted on amicable terms and as we left
we shook hands. As he gripped my hand I heard my bones
crunch. It was about three days before I could write with that
hand.

Andrew's father was a thoughtful person. At first he thought
all this 'psychology' was rubbish and wanted his boy to be
tough. He worried that teaching Andrew psychological techniques might make him a wimp. Yet he was ready to understand
that this was not necessarily so. It is possible to be competitive and stand up for yourself and still think about and feel for
others. In fact children who show more empathy do better at
school. They are better at analytical thinking and are more
creative.

Empathy involves recognising the feelings of others and
sharing those feelings. Empathy should not be associated
with weakness. A person can be empathic but still highly
competitive. It would be difficult to find a more fiercely competitive cricketer than Steve Waugh when he played for
Australia. Yet he also did a lot of work in India for poor children — and he did not boast about it either. In similar ways,
Ian Thorpe is very competitive and very successful, yet he too
is involved in charitable work. Many movie stars do a lot of
work for charity, but it would be difficult to think of a more
competitive and cut-throat industry than the one in which
they work. Mother Theresa was extraordinarily empathic, yet
she was also a very strong person.

Is it possible to be an empathic bouncer? Yes, I met one —
Andrew's dad. Someone who is kind to his family, who uses

his strong arms to pick up his children and help old ladies across the street, and who doesn't go looking for trouble, but who will, if it comes his way, use his strength, without going overboard. He just needs to learn to control his handshake.

Can we change society as Daniel Goleman thinks we can? Yes, but the change must start with children and come from families. If all parents were responsive to the needs of their children and brought them up to achieve as well as they can, to manage their destructive feelings, to resolve conflicts and think of others, it would make a difference. We've had the industrial revolution, and we've had the age of information technology; now it is time to start looking at our potential as human beings. This must start with our children.

... children who show more empathy do better at school. They are better at analytical thinking and are more creative.

Empathy is an important skill to teach children. As the example at the beginning of the chapter demonstrates, females are more likely than males to show empathy. Perhaps mothers are in the best position to teach children to put themselves in the other child's place and imagine how it feels. If a child can do this, she is less likely to be aggressive to others or to tease others.

By the age of three, children are able to recognise the feelings of others. They often smile when they see others are happy. It takes a little longer for children to distinguish other people's negative emotions, such as fear, anger and sadness. They usually learn to do this by the age of five. Below are some ways to teach children how to recognise emotions in others.

- **Encourage positive emotions.** Psychology tends to focus on controlling negative emotions rather than trying to encourage positive emotions. Books with titles such as *Control Your Depression*, *Beating the Blues*, and *Anger that Hurts* are everywhere. It is just as important, though, to encourage positive emotions. We can do this mostly by providing a warm, loving and happy environment. The techniques described in Chapters 4 and 5 will help you focus on positives, not negatives. We can give our children more positive messages through the way we talk. Rather than being overly critical of people, point out ways they might help others or do something good, such as give time to the school, be involved in the swimming club or coach cricket or football. Talking about good role models such as Steve Waugh and Ian Thorpe sends very positive messages to children.

- **Why is the other person feeling that way?** Recognising emotions in others is the first step; the next step is talking about *why* that person might be experiencing the emotion.

'That little boy has just lost his balloon. How do you think he feels?'

'It's James's birthday, how does he feel?'

'Karen has just done a beautiful painting. How do you think she is feeling?'

'You just took Brendan's toy! How do you think he feels?'

You might also remind children of how they felt at times when they were upset.

'That boy fell off his bike. You did that yesterday. How did you feel then?'

'Derek just broke his toy. Do you remember when your fire
truck broke? How did you feel? How do you think Derek feels?'

- **Be a good role model.** It is important for us as parents
  to model empathy in our dealings with others. If we can
  see things from the perspective of others and talk about
  this with our children this will help them learn.
- **Show empathy towards our own children.** By showing
  empathy towards our own children we are providing
  important modelling.
- **Pets can help develop children's empathy.** Having a
  pet is a good way to teach children empathy. We can
  use the emotions of the animal to help children learn
  the perspective of another living thing.

'I think the puppy knows we are going out — it's whining.
How do you think she feels?'

'She's wagging her tail. Do you think she's happy?'

- **Play helping games.** A doctor's kit is a good way to
  introduce helping responses. Also, try playing with
  ambulances, police cars and rescue service vehicles,
  and setting up hospitals. These are all times when you
  can talk about the feelings of others and how you can
  help people feel better.
- **Encourage empathy.** Give positive feedback for any
  displays of empathy or helping behaviour between siblings or between your child and her friends.

Teaching children to recognise the feelings of others and to
understand why they might be acting that way is an important skill. It can reduce anger and promote understanding.

Seeing the other person's point of view is a major step towards resolving conflict.

In a nutshell

- Recognising others' feelings can change the way we react and can reduce our angry feelings.
- Empathy should not be associated with weakness. Many tough and competitive people show considerable empathy.
- Talk to children about others in a positive way, and talk to them about how others might be feeling.
- Pets are good at bringing out empathy in children, as are playing doctors and emergency services.

14 Learning to relax

Anxiety affects one in ten children. It is the most common childhood psychological problem. Today's world is more complex, less secure and faster changing than the past. All children feel worried or scared at times, and all children need to learn to cope with worry or anxiety. Anxiety is in part inherited. In primitive times people who were sensitive to stress were good at avoiding danger, and this helped their chances of survival. A highly tuned fight or flight reaction was an asset. This sensitivity, which we now call anxiety, was passed down to future generations. Today, being constantly on the alert and sensitive to stress is not so useful. This means that sensitive people need to learn to control their natural stress reaction.

Children who have been abused are in a state of alert all the time. They live with danger and have to learn to survive it. Abused children do not put themselves at risk by going into deep sleep for too long at night. During sleep, we go through cycles from light sleep (from which we are more easily awoken) to deep sleep. In abused children, 'alerting' waves pulse through their brain to push them out of deep sleep into lighter sleep. Children from abusive families get less than one-third the deep sleep of other children.

Deep sleep is important for the development of a child. It is during deep sleep that the body's growth hormones are made and our immune system recovers. As a result of reduced deep sleep, abused children are often shorter than average and suffer more physical illnesses. Stress hormones also circulate continually in abused children, and this can slow brain development.

In some cases of child sexual assault the memory of the abuse may be suppressed, as it is too distressing. The memory of abuse is in the subconscious memory, but not the conscious. As the memory has been repressed, the child will feel fearful, but will not know why.

Relaxation

It is not easy to relax when we are under stress. The worst thing a doctor can say to me as he is flicking the air bubbles out of a large syringe with an enormous needle is, 'Now just relax.' I am too tense to relax.

For relaxation to be effective, it must be practised regularly, so that it dampens the overall level of anxiety inside us. Regular relaxation calms the nervous system. If we are more relaxed generally, when we are confronted with a fearful situation our anxiety levels do not go as high.

Relaxation exercises work best for children who are four years old or older. However, children vary considerably in their willingness to do relaxation exercises. Some children will practise every day, others will avoid it at all costs. Children are much more likely to practise if their parents do it with them. Try to find a regular time. It only takes ten minutes. Mornings are sometimes too big a rush — afternoons or evenings may work better.

Here are two relaxation exercises you can do with your child. They both take about ten minutes. The first is best for children aged from four to six. The second is better for older children. It is in the form of a script that you can read out to your child. Better still, make a recording and play it back, so that you can do the exercises with your child. You too will benefit from regular relaxation.

Anxiety affects one in ten children. It is the most common childhood psychological problem.

Relaxation exercises for young children (aged four to six)

Your child should lie down on his back with his arms at his sides. Here we go:

> Being relaxed means letting your body go loose and floppy, just like a rag doll. When you are relaxed, you feel very calm and peaceful and happy. Just lie down on your back, with your arms loosely at your sides. Close your eyes gently. Keep your eyes closed while we are doing the exercises.
>
> I want you to imagine that you have two dogs and that you are taking them for a walk in the garden. They are both on a lead and you have one lead in each hand. I want you to show me how you hold on to the leads nice and tightly.

Suddenly another dog wanders past your garden. Both your dogs try to run after him and pull at the leads. You must stop them running away and pull them back with all your might. Pull … pull harder now … pull as hard as you can. Phew! The other dog has gone away now and your dogs are no longer pulling. You can relax. *(Wait ten seconds.)*

Now I want you to pretend that your legs are like planks of wood. Make them go stiff and hard … Make them straight and hard … harder … harder still. Now relax them and feel them go soft and loose and floppy. *(Wait ten seconds.)*

Pretend that you are standing beside a lamp post. You look around the lamp post and see a fierce monster coming your way. If you run it will see you and chase you. There is nowhere to hide except behind the lamp post. But it is a very thin lamp post and you have to make yourself as skinny as you can, otherwise the monster will see you. Make yourself as thin as you can … thinner … thinner still. Phew! The monster has gone, so you can relax again. *(Wait ten seconds.)*

Now I want you to imagine that you are in the jungle. You are lying down relaxing after a hard walk. All of a sudden you hear a sound. Boom … boom … boom. The sound is getting closer and closer, and you look up to see a baby hippopotamus coming straight towards you. Baby hippos move very fast and you don't have time to get out of the way. So you make your stomach go stiff and hard, so that when the baby hippo steps on it, it won't hurt so much. Here it comes. Get ready, make your tummy go stiff and hard … harder … harder. Phew! It's turned away. Now you can relax your tummy. *(Wait ten seconds.)*

Now I want you to make an angry face. Scrunch up the muscles of your face. Make it as angry as you can. Notice how tense your face feels when it is angry. Now make a sad face. The muscles around your mouth tighten up and pull your mouth down into a frown. It doesn't feel very relaxed. Now just relax with a lovely gentle smile on your face. Your face feels nice and relaxed.

Now let's practise breathing nice and slowly. It is important to breathe gently, deeply and slowly when relaxing. When I tell you, I want you to breathe in slowly, deeply and gently. Hold your breath while I count to five, then breathe out again, slowly and gently. Are you ready?

Breathe in, slowly and gently ... 1 ... 2 ... 3 ... 4 ... 5 ... Breathe out slowly and gently. *(Repeat breathing in and out four times.)*

Now I want you to carry on breathing slowly and gently. *(Wait one minute.)*

Now when I count to three, I want you to open your eyes. You will feel awake but fully relaxed ... 1 ... 2 ... 3 ... Open your eyes.

Relaxation exercise for older children

As with the previous exercise, your child should lie down on his back with his arms at his side. Read out the following in an unhurried soothing voice:

To relax means to let your body go loose and soft and floppy, just like a rag doll. When you are relaxed, you feel very calm and peaceful and happy. Just lie down on your back, with your arms loosely at your sides. Close your eyes gently. Keep them closed during the exercises.

You are going to practise tightening up your body and then relaxing your body. This will help you learn the difference between when your body is tight and tense and when your body is soft and relaxed. When I tell you, I want you to start tightening up each part of your body in turn.

First of all curl up your toes ... curl them up as tightly as you can. Now make your legs go stiff and hard, just like planks of wood ... make them really stiff ... harder ... harder ... That's good.

Now pull in your tummy ... tighten up your tummy as much as you can ... pull it right in. Tighten the muscles of your chest now ... notice that it is difficult to breathe easily and freely if your chest muscles are tight.

Now make your arms go stiff and hard and clench your hands into a fist. Harder ... harder ... make your arms stiffer and really clench your fist as tight as you can. Finally, make an angry face ... screw your face up in anger.

Your whole body now is stiff and hard and tense. All your muscles are tight. Make your whole body tighter and tighter.

Now take in a deep breath and hold it. *(Wait five seconds.)*

Now breathe out slowly. As you breathe out, let your whole body relax. Let all your muscles relax.

Stop curling up your toes. Let them go loose and floppy. Let your legs relax ... stop stiffening them, and just let them rest gently on the floor.

Let your tummy go soft and relax your chest. Let your arms go soft and floppy ... let your hands lie gently open. Let all the muscles of your face relax.

Your whole body is loose and soft and relaxed now. Your body might feel warm, heavy and relaxed.

Now let's practise breathing nice and slowly. It is important to breathe gently, deeply and slowly when relaxing. When I tell you I want you to breathe in slowly, deeply and gently. Hold your breath while I count to five, then breathe out again, slowly and gently. Are you ready?

Breathe in, slowly and gently ... 1 ... 2 ... 3 ... 4 ... 5 ... breathe out slowly and gently. *(Repeat breathing in and out slowly four times.)*

Now I am going to give you a word to say each time you breathe out. As you breathe out I want you to say 'Calm' silently to yourself. Say it each time you breathe out. Carry on breathing gently, slowly and deeply, and each time you breathe out say 'Calm'. *(Wait one minute.)*

Now when I count to three, I want you to open your eyes. You will feel awake but fully relaxed ... 1 ... 2 ... 3 ... Open your eyes.

Visualisations

Some children find that imagining a peaceful scene enhances their state of relaxation. After doing the relaxation exercises, ask them to think of somewhere they feel very relaxed and ask them to imagine, with their eyes still closed, that they are actually there. Ask them to see all the colours, hear all the sounds and smell all the smells.

Alternatively, take them through a scene you know they will like. You might start a visualisation like this:

Imagine that you are lying on the grass by a mountain stream looking up at a snow-capped mountain. Although the mountain still has snow on its peak, down where you are it is a warm, sunny day. The mountain stream is bubbling in front of you and the water is crystal clear. You can see fish darting and dancing in the water.

You look up at the mountain towering above you and the snow at the top glistening in the sunlight. You might climb it one day. You see a solitary eagle circling in the sky. It rides the air currents gracefully.

The soothing sounds of the mountain stream blend with the peaceful view of the mountain to make you feel very relaxed and pleasant. You don't have a care in the world and you know that you can always think of this place and you will feel calm.

Many children find beach scenes relaxing. If you have a favourite beach that you go to you can add some details of it in the description below.

Imagine that we are staying at a beautiful cottage on the beach. It is a pretty blue cottage with a tin roof. It is right on the beach and there are no other houses or people around. You walk out the door and you are on the beach. You feel the soft sand on your feet. It is a beautiful day and the sea is bright blue. The waves are rolling in and you can hear the gentle sound as they break on the beach. You hear the seagulls squawking and see them gliding in the sky. You reach the sea and the waves gently lap at your bare feet — it feels good, and cools you down.

There are many books and audiotapes of visualisations (see Further reading).

Relaxation can be combined to great effect with some of the techniques described in the next chapter. I was seeing an eight-year-old boy, Brad, whose father had been in a serious car accident (fortunately, he recovered fully). After the accident, whenever Brad's parents went out he would panic. They could not go anywhere or leave him with anyone.

When Brad and his family came to see me, I gave him some relaxation exercises to practise for two weeks. Then I asked him to come up with a phrase to think while his parents were out (there is more on this in the next chapter). Brad was a *Lord of the Rings* fan, and we talked about what his hero, Legolas, might tell himself. Brad decided on the phrase, 'I'll be brave, I'll be strong' if he became fearful.

It is critical with childhood fears to work gradually. Each step was discussed with Brad and we talked about what Brad thought he could manage. He said he thought he would be all right if his parents went out for two hours (while Brad was looked after by someone he liked), but not too far away.

Brad practised his relaxation every day. Just before his parents went out he relaxed again and practised his breathing. We also made sure there were plenty of distractions to take his mind off his fear. So he was allowed to hire a computer game and a DVD.

Gradually the parents increased the time they went out and the distance they went — but they only increased it by what Brad thought he could handle. Soon they were back to normal.

Relaxation exercises are most effective if they are practised every day; it often takes around two weeks before they have a noticeable effect. And remember, some children really enjoy relaxation exercises and enjoy the pleasant feelings that it produces, but other children are not so keen. Encourage your children, but do not force them to practise. Try to practise with them. If they still resist, try some of the methods in the next chapter.

In a nutshell

- Anxiety affects one in ten children.
- Regular relaxation exercises can lower your child's overall level of anxiety.
- Visualisations can enhance a child's feeling of relaxation.
- For relaxation exercises to work best, they must be practised daily (don't expect any change for the first two weeks).
- Some children do not like relaxation exercises. Do not force them to do them.

Some other ways to reduce anxiety

Relaxation exercises can be very useful, but other techniques can greatly increase the effects of relaxation. The techniques described below can be used with relaxation exercises — or instead of them, if your child is one of those who does not enjoy relaxation exercises.

Taming the fear monster

In Chapter 3 we discussed the strategy of separating the problem from the child by 'objectifying' the problem. This means giving the problem a name. Then the child is not the problem, the problem is the problem, and the problem is something the whole family (including the child) can work against. This works very well for fears (revisit Chapter 3 if necessary, where the technique is described in detail).

> Belinda was eight years old. Her parents had trouble getting her to bed, and when she was in bed, she did not go to sleep until after 11.00 pm. As a result she was tired and irritable during the

day and had trouble concentrating at school. She had fears about burglars coming into the house at night. We talked about the fear inside her that was stopping her get to sleep. Belinda decided to call her fear the Scary Monster, and she drew a very frightening monster indeed. We talked about the Scary Monster and how sneaky it was — after all, it waited for the dark, when Belinda was on her own in bed. We talked about how stupid the monster was, because most robberies occur in the daytime and the Scary Monster was getting it all wrong by only coming out at night.

We talked about how the Scary Monster didn't like it when Belinda was brave and relaxed. And he really didn't like it when Belinda thought about other things in bed. So we taught Belinda some relaxation exercises and got her to think about how brave she was, and to say to herself, 'I'll be brave' instead of being scared. We talked to Belinda about how this would make the Scary Monster so weak that he would give up and go some-where else.

Using these methods, in a few weeks Belinda was going to bed happily — and was asleep by 8.30 pm.

Self-talk

When we are in a stressful or scary situation we are constantly thinking or talking to ourselves: 'Oh no, I think the boss heard me say that. I'm in trouble now. Why don't I learn to keep my mouth shut?', for example. Children, although they do not usually realise it, also talk to themselves when they encounter something stressful. Often the difference between a child who copes well with the situation and a child who has diffi-culty is what she thinks or says to herself. For example, suppose a child has to give a talk in front of her class. An anxious child may think:

> I really hate giving talks. I get nervous and will probably say something silly and everyone will laugh at me. It's going to be terrible.

By thinking these thoughts, the anxious child might tense herself up so much that she might not do as well as she could. Compare this with another child, who thinks:

> It is hard to stand up in front of everyone. Everyone gets a bit nervous. But it will not take long, and the teacher said I did well last time and I was pleased with myself. I'll be fine.

This child is likely to cope much better, because she is giving herself more positive messages. The difference between a child who copes well with situations and one who is fearful is often how the child *thinks* about the situation.

To illustrate just how much your thoughts affect how your body feels, just close your eyes for a moment and think of something unpleasant that has happened to you in the past. Think about it as clearly as you can. Watch the events unfold and focus on every detail in your memory. Now open your eyes and notice how your body feels. Usually your body feels unpleasant: in the words of one child I did this with, it just makes you feel 'Yuk'.

Now think of something very pleasant. It might be your favourite place, such as the beach, or just sitting in the garden, or somewhere special you have been that you will always remember. Close your eyes and imagine the scene as vividly as you can — the colours, the sounds and the smells. Stay with it for a moment to get rid of the unpleasant sensations from the last image. When you open your eyes you will notice how much better you feel.

This exercise shows how much our thoughts influence how we feel physically. If we are thinking of positive images, we feel much better in our body than if we focus on negative thoughts. It follows that by changing the way we think, we can change the way we feel physically.

One way children can be taught to change the way they are thinking is by getting them to talk to themselves in a much more positive way. Psychologists call the way we talk to ourselves about things — you guessed it — 'self-talk'. If children can use positive self-talk in frightening situations it can make a difference to how they feel.

Self-talk involves asking children to think of a phrase that makes them feel better in a stressful situation, and then say this phrase over and over quietly to themselves when they feel stressed.

In my work as a clinical psychologist I have seen many parents who have been an inspiration. I have worked with parents who have had children with serious, sometimes terminal, illnesses. I have supported parents who have had children with physical disabilities, or developmental delays, or who are autistic. Such children require a much higher degree of care, and often parents cannot leave their children for long, and they cannot put their child in day care. The children require hospitalisations, tests, visits to specialists and lots and lots of extra work. The parents I have seen have given all that is required and more.

Working with these families, I have often asked myself how I would react in similar circumstances. The answer is that I simply do not know. We, as health professionals, see the disability or illness; they, as parents, see the child.

Almost without exception, due to the work and dedication of the parents, the children did substantially better than expected. These parents are the unsung heroes of our society. I remember one case, in particular, because it was the first time I used self-talk with a young child.

I was seeing a three-year-old, Josh, who had severe juvenile arthritis. His joints were inflamed, swollen and red. His movements were severely restricted and any movement was very painful. However, for arthritis, movement is the therapy — otherwise the joints will deteriorate. When the condition had flared up at its worst, Josh's mother was instructed by the medical staff to give him 20 minutes of physiotherapy exercises three times a day. The problem for Josh and his mother was that this was 20 minutes of pain. Josh, of course, had no concept that the exercise would make him feel better in the long run. To him, it just hurt, and to make things worse, it was his mother who was doing it to him. Every physio session his mother attempted was a battle with tantrums, screams and tears. Instead of 20 minutes, it was taking Josh's mother well over an hour to get through the required exercises. This was happening three times a day and was placing a severe strain on their relationship.

The difference between a child who copes well with situations and one who is fearful is often how the child *thinks* about the situation.

I worked with Josh's mother, who was very distressed at causing him more pain, but was also determined to help him. Josh was too young to tell us what he was thinking during the physiotherapy exercises, but it was not too difficult to imagine that he was not thinking pleasant thoughts. Josh was very bright, and we told him we wanted him to choose a short phrase that he could say to himself while his mum was doing the exercises. We gave him some suggestions, including 'I'll be brave' or 'I can do it', but these did not feel right for him. Josh and his mum came up with 'All over soon', and he liked this. So when it was time for the exercises he would say to himself 'All over soon.'

We started with a few minutes of physio, timed with a timer. In this time Josh distracted himself by saying 'All over soon' over and over again. Gradually we built the time up to the required 20 minutes.

I asked Josh's mum to keep going through the cries, which was very hard, but he got a big cuddle at the end. Within a couple of weeks, Josh's mum was getting through all the required exercises in the 20 minutes, three times a day. Josh's crying and distress were much less. Josh did very well. So did his parents.

Using self-talk is a useful tool to help children (and adults) overcome fears. It blocks all those unwanted negative thoughts that the fear feeds on and that make the fear worse. It is best if your child can come up with her own phrase to say quietly to herself when she is afraid. Your child should take a deep breath, then repeat the phrase over and over. If your child cannot come up with a phrase, here are a few suggestions:

'I'll be brave.'

'I can do it.'

'I'm strong.'

'I'm tough.'

'I'll beat it.'

And, of course, my favourite, 'All over soon.'

Another way to encourage positive self-talk is to get your child to think about one of her favourite heroes. It might be Spiderman or Harry Potter or Aragorn or a sports star or a pop singer. Whoever your child likes at the moment. You might ask, 'What would Harry Potter do? What do you think he would say to himself if he was scared?'

Modelling

Parents can also show their children how *they* cope with stressful situations. We all have situations which make us nervous, but many parents do not talk about these to their children. If parents can show their child some of their own coping skills, it can make a difference. I give many lectures in my work, often to audiences of 100 people or more. No matter how many I do, I still get nervous before each one. I am forever indebted to Josh, the three-year-old with juvenile rheumatoid arthritis, for coming up with the self-talk phrase that gets me through these. As I am giving the lecture I glance up at the clock and think 'All over soon.' I have no problem telling my children, when they are worried about giving a presentation at school, that this is how I get through. Being a good model for your children doesn't mean you have to cope perfectly yourself, as the following example shows.

> When I was working in a large teaching hospital, I was seeing a young girl, Carly. She was about twelve, and had just been diagnosed with diabetes. This involved giving herself injections of insulin regularly. The problem was that she had a very severe phobia about injections and none of the doctors could overcome it.

As part of the treatment program, I felt Carly needed a model to cope with the injections. As none of my colleagues volunteered, it was up to me. We talked about the fact that I also did not like injections, but we would go through some techniques of relaxation and self-talk, then I would use these to cope with having an injection. Then it would be Carly's turn. I must admit that it hurt, and I did not enjoy it, and Carly laughed at me. Still, it worked, and she herself had an injection straight afterwards.

I rationalised to myself afterwards that it was much better that I did not cope too well. The research on being a good model shows that children have trouble relating to a model who copes perfectly. The best models are those who show some fear, but overcome it. I'm fairly sure I showed enough human frailty for any child, and at least I pretended to overcome it.

This is probably why many of the most successful books and movies show heroes struggling at first and repeatedly failing before finally overcoming adversity when it really matters. Harry Potter, *Lord of the Rings* and Spiderman are all examples of this. We can identify with these characters.

Breathing

When we become tense, we breathe shallowly and quickly, often through our mouths. One of the surest ways to calm down is to focus on our breathing and slow it down. By slowing down our breathing we can induce a sense of relaxation. In fact certain yoga people say that if we reduce our respiration rate to less than four times a minute we induce an automatic state of meditation.

While regular daily relaxation can lower the body's overall level of anxiety, controlling our breathing can be used to calm ourselves down very quickly in tense situations. If you practise it enough, it can act something like a 'rescue remedy'. Here are three breathing methods that can be used by children and adults.

Deep breathing

Ask your child to pretend she is a big balloon. Ask her to take a deep breath and fill the balloon with as much air as she can. Then slowly let the air out. Ask her to listen to the sounds of the air as it comes out of her mouth.

Repeat three times. As she breathes in, ask her to do it as slowly as possible so as not to burst the balloon. As she breathes out she can say 'Calm' to herself (or 'Relax').

Model this for your child and practise at bedtime before your child goes to sleep. Also use it when your child is upset.

Karate breathing

Karate breathing is a good breathing technique, and boys like it because it sounds tough. You can explain that it is used by karate champions when they want to be calm before a championship fight. Demonstrate this for your child first, so that she can copy what you do:

- Take a deep, *slow* breath in through the nose.
- Hold the breath in the tummy for a few seconds.
- Breathe out slowly through the mouth.
- Repeat three times.

Yoga breathing

Yoga breathing focuses on breathing using the diaphragm (a dome-shaped membrane separating the lungs from the abdomen). When the diaphragm compresses downwards it pulls air into the lungs. Chest muscles are also involved in breathing, but if only chest muscles are used, breathing is shallow.

With your child lying on her back, ask her to put one hand on her tummy and the other hand on her chest. Ask her to breathe in slowly through her tummy so that the hand on her tummy rises up first. (To do this her diaphragm will move downwards.) As she continues to breathe in fully, the hand on her chest will rise up too.

As she breathes out, the hand on her chest should go down first as the air is expelled from the chest. Then the hand on her tummy will go down as the air is expelled out of her lower lungs by the diaphragm rising up and pushing the air out.

It might sound complicated, but all you and your child need to focus on is her hands going up and down. For breathing in, the hand on the tummy should rise first, then the hand on the chest. For breathing out, the hand on the chest should go down first, followed by the hand on the tummy.

It is best to demonstrate this to your child first.

Gradually ask your child to breathe in and out more slowly. You have just taught her yoga breathing, which is very beneficial psychologically as well as healthwise.

Breathing methods are an effective addition to self-talk. If your child is anxious, get her to take three deep breaths to calm down and then practise her self-talk.

Exercise

When we are stressed, our body is in fight or flight mode. The heart is pumping, the breathing rate increases — our body is primed for action. Trying to relax while your body is in this state can be difficult because, in a sense, trying to relax is going against the tide. The most effective thing to do when you are stressed is to exercise, *then* relax. This works the adrenaline (which is released by the fight or flight response) out of the system.

Aerobic exercise is good for stress release. Aerobic exercise increases the efficiency of the body's intake of oxygen by increasing heart and lung activity. Good forms of aerobic exercise for children are:

- going for a walk
- bike riding
- trampolining
- jogging
- soccer
- football

- tennis
- volleyball
- netball.

Relaxation exercises after this can then get the body into a very deep state of relaxation. A regular routine of daily exercise followed by ten minutes of relaxation can have very beneficial results in about two weeks. If you do it with your child, you will benefit too.

If your child has serious problems with anxiety or phobias, get some counselling. Alternatively, try reading *Keys to Parenting Your Anxious Child* by Katharina Manassis or *Helping Your Anxious Child* by Ron Rapee and his colleagues (see Further reading).

In a nutshell

- Separating the fear from the child can help tame the fear monster.
- Self-talk is an effective way to deal with negative thoughts.
- Breathing methods can help when your child is in a stressful situation.
- Exercise followed by relaxation exercises can induce a state of deep calmness.

16 Helping children solve problems

'I wanted to watch *The Simpsons*,' says Tom.

'Go and watch it on the other TV. I'm watching my show,' Alicia says.

'Dad's watching the news. I want to watch *The Simpsons* now,' Tom replies.

Some children are playing cricket. Lachlan, the batsman, hits the ball and runs. At the other end Robert grabs the ball and aims at the stumps. Lachlan slides into the crease. The bails fly off the stumps. It is a very close call.

'I was in,' says Lachlan.

'You were out,' says Robert.

'I wasn't.'

'Were so.'

Sophie has Brianna over to play. Sophie spends her whole time playing with her new Barbie. Brianna wants to play something else. They get angry with each other and both go off sulking.

Conflicts occur every day, and can be a source of frustration for children and adults alike. Children who cannot solve problems often escalate the conflict. We saw in the very first example in Chapter 1 how Ben had trouble coming up with alternatives to aggressive behaviour. If children become aggressive and emotional whenever a conflict arises, they are likely to be rejected by other children. Children who can solve problems, on the other hand, are more popular, and better able to cope in a variety of situations. Children who can stay calm, think of different solutions and think ahead are likely to get on better with other children and adults.

Problem solving is an important skill, but it is a long-term strategy. Parents can coach their children in problem-solving skills from an early age (about four) through to the end of high school. Children (and many adults) can take a long time to get the hang of problem-solving skills. However, if they practise from an early age, when they are older it becomes second nature to use these skills for the increasingly complex situations they will face.

Young children can learn simple problem-solving steps. Two-year-olds think mainly of themselves and only see things from their own point of view. They want an outcome that satisfies only their needs.

At this stage, any problem solving needs to be very basic. The first step is to set limits on any inappropriate behaviour. Particularly, stop any hurtful behaviour: 'Stop hitting Abby — it hurts her.' This lets the child know that it is not all right to hit and it helps him learn how the other child feels. Teach the skills of sharing and taking turns described in Chapter 11. This lays the basis of future problem solving.

By the age of three, children's language is improving rapidly, and they talk and chat much more. This increase in communication also results in more arguments and quarrels. Children at this age still tend to be inflexible, and focused on themselves. 'No. It's mine!' is the most common outcome of attempted negotiation (I know many adults who have not got beyond this stage).

By the age of four, children can learn more flexible problem-solving strategies. They can start to understand the needs of others, and they can start to argue their case and listen to reason (but they can also resort to threats and aggression).

By the age of five, children can see things from another's point of view and work out solutions that are best for both parties, although this does not always happen.

There is also considerable difference between children. For example, children who have found that aggression has worked well in the past tend to try to dominate others into submission. Other children might tend to give in to others.

Problem solving builds on many of the skills already covered in this book, and also brings them together. Your child will master the problem-solving steps more quickly if he can:

- take turns and share (Chapter 11)
- begin to recognise his feelings (Chapter 12) and calm himself down (Chapters 14 and 15)
- listen (Chapter 10), and see things from the other person's point of view (Chapter 13).

Here are the five steps for teaching your child how to solve problems. You can start when your children are as young as three, but they may not grasp the steps until they are four or five.

Step 1: What is the problem?

Our natural inclination is to jump into any conflict between children and try to solve it, even though we probably did not see everything that went on. This does not help children learn to solve their own problems. Instead of doing this, wait and ask the children to describe the problem. Ask each child in turn and remember your listening skills (Chapter 10). Listen carefully, then summarise the main points.

Dad: 'Okay, what happened? You first, Alicia.'

Alicia: 'I was watching my show and Tom wanted to watch *The Simpsons*. I told him to watch it on the other television.'

Dad: 'Tom?'

Tom: 'Dad, you were watching the other television. She watched her show yesterday and I missed mine then. It's not fair.'

Alicia: 'But you watched it all last week!'

Dad: 'Okay, so the two of you wanted to watch different programs. Tom, you said the same thing happened last night. Alicia, you said Tom watched *The Simpsons* every day last week.'

Step 2: How do you feel?

The second step has two parts. The first part is to try to get the children to recognise their own feelings. The second part is to ask each child how they think the *other* child is feeling. Doing this helps them learn that it is not just them who feel aggrieved.

Dad: 'How do you feel, Tom?'

Tom: 'ANGRY!'

Dad: 'Alicia?'

Alicia (angrily): 'Okay, let him watch it. He always gets his own way!'

Dad: 'No, I'm asking you how you feel.'

Alicia: 'Annoyed! I'm missing my show!'

Step 3: Calming down

Anger prevents problem solving. When we get angry, instead of looking for solutions, we often spend our time going over and over why *we* are right and the other person is wrong. We try to justify our behaviour by saying things like, 'He always gets his own way', or, 'I never get to watch what I want. It's not fair!' Once we get trapped into this way of thinking, it can go round and round in a loop, which we never get out of.

Chapters 14 and 15 described some ways children (and adults) can calm themselves down; these can be useful for reducing anger. The breathing techniques in Chapter 15 can be especially useful in this situation.

'Let's all take three deep breaths and calm down. Remember, breathe in through the nose and out through the mouth. Nice deep breaths, ready? Breathe in … hold it. Count to three. One … two … three. Again …'

Step 4: Alternative solutions

We all like our own solutions best, so encourage your children to come up with their own solutions. Children are more likely to accept a solution if *they* — not you — suggested it. So even if you think you know the perfect solution, stay quiet for a while and see what they come up with. Then you can make suggestions.

Give them time. At first they might not be able to think of things and you may have to make some suggestions. However, if you get them to problem solve on a regular basis, they will soon become good at coming up with ideas. I regularly run groups for four-year-olds on problem solving. I use puppets to act out a problem situation. In one scenario, the puppets both grab hold of the same toy and fight over it. When I first ask the four-year-olds for suggestions about what the puppets might do instead of fighting there is often silence. When they have had a bit of practice and get the hang of it they usually come up with so many ideas I cannot get a word in.

Returning to our television dispute:

Dad 'Let's see. Can either of you think of a way we could solve this problem with the television?

Alicia: 'Get another television.'

Dad: 'Any other ideas?'

Tom: 'Dad can watch the late news.'

Dad: 'Any other suggestions?'

Alicia: 'Take turns?'

Tom: 'Then I'll miss all my favourite episodes.'

Alicia: 'We could record Tom's show and he could watch it later.'

Tom: 'We could record your show, you mean.'

Alicia: 'Okay, we could take turns. I could tape my show one night.'

Tom: 'Dad could tape the news every night, then we could both watch our shows!'

It is important that you encourage the children to think of as many solutions as possible at this stage, and do not dismiss any that are suggested — this is a brainstorming session, really. If you start to say that some of the ideas are silly, the children will be discouraged. Allow the ideas to flow and they will become more creative.

Step 5: Ask the children to work out the best solution

You have let the children come up with a number of solutions without passing judgement on any of the ideas. Now the children need to think ahead, to think their ideas through, and judge which solution will bring about the best results for everybody. Of course some ideas are simply not acceptable — now is the time to let them know about those ones.

> Dad: 'Let's look more closely at the ideas. First, we cannot afford another television. Second, I'm not going to record the news every night. You came up with some really good other ideas, though — let's look at those.'
>
> Alicia: 'I suppose we could take turns.'
>
> Dad: 'Do you think that would work?'
>
> Tom: 'I think we'd argue. Taking turns recording the shows would be best.'
>
> Dad: 'How would you take turns recording — would you alternate nightly or week by week?
>
> Alicia: 'Nightly.'
>
> Tom: 'Yeah, nightly.'
>
> Alicia: 'Let's make up a roster.'

These steps may seem awkward at first but, remember, you are coaching them in a skill that they will use for life. Be patient — they will eventually learn to solve their own problems through reason, not anger.

When not to use problem solving

There are times to do problem solving and times not to do it. If your child is upset and cranky, he will not listen. If your children are fighting, it is best to send them to time-out (see Chapter 7) rather than attempt to problem solve straight away. This shows them that there are limits to how they can behave.

Later, when things are calm, you can discuss what happened. You can start by saying that you want to avoid a recurrence of the fighting. You can then go through the incident and use the problem-solving steps to encourage the children to come up with solutions.

> Mum: 'Okay, Lachlan and Robert, you had an argument when you were playing cricket and got into a fight. What happened then?'
>
> Lachlan: 'You made us stop playing and sent us both to time-out.'
>
> Mum: 'So did you choose a good solution to your argument?'
>
> Lachlan and Robert: 'No.'
>
> Mum: 'What else could you have done?'

Problem solving can also be effective if you get in early, before the conflict gets out of hand. Then you can use the problem-solving steps before emotions take over. If Mum had seen the cricket incident, for instance, she might have intervened before the fight started and used the problem-solving steps then.

Traffic lights

Some people use a picture of traffic lights for problem solving — it gives a visual picture of the problem-solving steps. Children can draw a picture of traffic lights and put it on their bedroom door.

RED	**STOP**	What is the problem?
		How do I feel?
		Take three deep breaths and calm down.
ORANGE	**THINK**	Think of alternative solutions.
		Think what would happen for each solution.
GREEN	**GO**	Pick the best solution and do it.

I was talking with my daughter, then only two and a half, about the city (we live in the country).

Nicola: 'It's busy in the city, isn't it? They have traffic lights in the city, don't they? They have colours, don't they? Red, green … what's the other one?'

Me (thankful to get a word in): 'Orange.'

Nicola: 'Oh yes, orange. Red is for stop, green is for go and orange is for … please yourself!'

In a nutshell

- The first step in problem solving is to ask the children 'What is the problem?'
- The second step is to find out how each one feels.
- The third step is to get them to calm down by taking three deep breaths.
- The fourth step is to help them come up with some creative solutions.
- The fifth step is to help them choose the best solution, by looking at how each solution will turn out in practice.

Teaching assertiveness

Debbie was playing in the sandpit with the sand-digger. Along came Jake. 'Gimme the digger,' he said loudly. He pushed Debbie away and started playing with it. Debbie moved away and started crying. She went to the teacher, who took her back to the sandpit. 'Jake, Debbie can play with the toys too. You must share.' But Debbie did not want to play near Jake — she went off to play somewhere else.

Assertiveness means expressing one's feelings and standing up for one's rights while respecting the feelings and rights of others. In the example above, neither Jake nor Debbie was assertive. Jake stood up for himself, but did not respect Debbie. Debbie did not stand up for herself; she just gave in.

Unfortunately, our children will encounter many situations like this — and much worse. Children are much more likely than adults to find themselves in situations in which other children grab things from them, hit them or are rude to them and tease them. These situations are everyday events at playgroups, preschools and schools. Alternatively, though we might not want to hear about it, it could be our child who is the aggressor.

Aggression is often 'rewarded': 80 percent of all aggressive acts between young children (up to five) are 'rewarded' by their victims being submissive and giving up objects. Aggressive children do not pick on others at random. Research indicates that aggressive children are more likely to pick on children they can make cry — it makes them feel powerful. They pick on children who are often alone, and who are likely to give in to them. They also pick on children who are very emotional and provide some kind of reaction.

Parents and teachers are more likely to be tolerant of aggression in boys. 'Oh, he's just a boy,' they say. In Chapter 13 we saw one example — the bouncer's son who was encouraged to learn to fight and be tough.

We are also more likely to encourage submission and acquiescence in girls. In one study, mothers told their daughters to give something up during play three times more often than they told their sons to give up something. In today's world we expect women to compete with men directly for jobs and careers. Teaching girls to be submissive is not the best way to equip them for this task.

It would be more helpful if we taught both boys and girls to be assertive. Assertiveness can replace excess aggression in boys and unwanted submissiveness in girls. Assertiveness is also necessary if we want our children to be able to resist peer pressure — in later life it is inevitable that they will be pressured to take drugs, and/or to drink too much, and/or to participate in unwanted sexual activity and/or to do something dangerous (such as drinking and driving or other criminal acts).

What is assertiveness?

Imagine you have just popped into the supermarket for one item. You are running late and have to pick the children up from school. Someone steps in front of you at the checkout queue. They may not have meant to — they might be in a world of their own and did not notice that you were there. There are three ways in which you can respond:

1 **Be passive.** Do nothing, but seethe about how it is making you late, especially when one of their items fails to scan and the checkout person has to find someone to get a price check, which takes ages!

2 **Be aggressive.** Get mad. Say in a very loud voice, 'THESE X!Y*Z* PEOPLE WHO THINK THEY ARE BETTER THAN ANYONE ELSE AND CAN JUST PUSH THEIR WAY IN!' You've lost the moral high ground.

> Assertiveness can replace excess aggression in boys and unwanted submissiveness in girls. Assertiveness is also necessary if we want our children to be able to resist peer pressure.

3 **Be assertive.** Respect others, but respect your rights too. Say in a clear voice, 'Excuse me, I think I was next.'

There are several things you need to do to be assertive:

1 Stay calm and do not let yourself become angry.
2 Look at the person you are speaking to.
3 Use an 'I' statement. 'You' statements often sound like accusations. Rather than saying, 'You pushed in', say 'I was next.'

4   Speak in a clear voice that is not soft, but is not loud
    and angry either.
5   Keep it brief.

Many adults are not assertive, which means they are not providing the best modelling for their children. Some adults
either do not speak up for themselves; at the other extreme
are those who think assertiveness is interrupting you halfway
through a sentence to tell you in a very loud voice how wrong
you are and how clever they are.

Assertiveness doesn't only apply to situations like the
supermarket example. It also means things like stopping and
asking for directions rather than getting lost. (Although being
male, I like to slow down so my wife can ask for directions
and model assertive behaviour to our children. Then I can sit
back and look as if I knew all along we had been going in completely the wrong direction for the last 60 kilometres.)

Assertiveness and sibling conflict

Few childhood relationships are as intense and conflict-
ridden as sibling relationships. All parents want their children
to get along with each other, but often we do not know how to
deal with these squabbles. Experts often add to the confusion
by advising parents to let their children sort it out by themselves. That way, it is argued, the children will learn to solve
their own problems.

Unfortunately, if children are left to sort things out for
themselves it is the stronger (usually, but not always, the older
or oldest) child who dominates. This sets up a pattern where
one child dominates and learns that aggression pays and the

other learns to be a victim. This is why many leaders are first-borns — one of their most refined skills is bossing everyone around. But these patterns can sow the seeds for feelings of hostility, inadequacy and incompetence in the victim.

The trouble is that when parents do intervene, they often take the younger child's side, telling the older one, 'You're older, you should know better.' This invites the younger sibling to tell on their older brother or sister, and most younger children do not need an invitation to do this.

If sibling conflict is an ongoing problem, the first step is to use an effective behaviour management strategy. The techniques described in Part 1 of this book should help. Remember, it is pointless trying to find out who started whatever it was — just use the same discipline methods for both children. It takes two to fight.

Then, when the children have finished time-out, use problem solving to prevent further squabbles. Teaching both children to be assertive rather than aggressive can give them alternative ways of behaving.

For example, Liam grabs a toy that Sara is playing with. Sara just gives up the toy, but sobs loudly, expecting sympathy and a cuddle (she's a victim, after all). Instead of giving her that, you might prompt an assertive response this way.

You: 'Did you want Liam to snatch that toy?'

Sara: 'No.'

You: 'Well, what could you do instead of just letting him take it?'

Sara: 'Grab it back?'

You: 'What do you think would happen then?'

Sara: 'Liam would probably hit me.'

You: 'What else could you do?'

Sara (after some thought): 'I don't know.'

You: 'What about just saying, "No, I was playing with that" in a clear voice? Let's practise that.'

The problem-solving steps can also be used for Liam. Liam needs to learn assertive behaviour instead of aggressive behaviour.

You: 'Liam, if you wanted the toy, what else could you have done besides snatching it?

Liam: 'Ask, I suppose.'

You: 'Okay, let's practise asking nicely. Remember, it's Sara's toy, so if she wants to keep playing with it, she can.'

As far as responding to dobbing goes, you can make it a rule not to become involved if children dob. Instead, you might use it as an opportunity to teach problem solving (for children four years and older). You might say, 'What do you think you could do when your brother says that?' Of course you should always make it clear to the child that she should tell you about things that may be very dangerous.

A frequent pattern of sibling conflict is when the older child becomes jealous of the younger child for getting a lot of *her* attention. Like an established employee in a work situation, she lets the new upstart know her place — which is at the bottom. At first the younger child accepts her fate, but not for long.

After a while the younger child retaliates, and she soon learns how to tease and provoke her older sibling. The older sibling inevitably reacts and gets into trouble, which leads to a smug self-satisfied look on the younger sibling's face. The older child then looks out for the next opportunity for revenge.

Studies show that squabbles between a preschooler and her toddler sibling occur about seven times an hour! (The fights do become less frequent as the children get older.)

Frank Sulloway argues that sibling rivalry is 'in the genes', and is to do with the survival of the fittest. Before the industrial revolution, families were much larger, times were much tougher and many children died before they reached their teens. Sulloway argues that parents only had so much time, money and food. Children who were successful in competing for these very limited resources did far better than the others. Thus the fittest and most competitive children survived and passed on their genes to future generations.

So the next time your child gets out the weighing scales to make sure she got as much cake as her brother ...

Sibling conflict is not necessarily bad. It is only when the fighting is extreme and one-sided that it can become a training ground for aggression. Studies show that if there is a balance between siblings supporting each other and fighting with each other, the children turn out to be better adjusted socially.

My two children never cease to amaze me: they can at times dislike one another intensely and be thoroughly horrible to each other, but there are also those other, beautiful times when they are helping each other or doing something together. And many parents tell me that the older brother treats his younger sibling mercilessly at home, but if anyone at school picks on little brother, his older sibling is fiercely protective.

Assertiveness for teasing and bullying

I find teaching problem-solving skills and assertiveness very useful for helping children who are being teased and bullied. If someone is teasing your child, try to find out exactly what is happening.

- Is it happening occasionally or every day?
- What is the other child (or children) doing or saying? If she is calling your child names, what exactly is she saying?
- How does your child react? If she says, 'Nothing, I ignore it' — most children will say they do this, but in practice it rarely happens — probe further using these questions:

    'Do you get upset?'

    'What do you do when you get upset?'

    'Do you sometimes answer back?'

Then go through the problem-solving steps (see Chapter 16). Most children come up with three main solutions.

1 Assertive talk. Say in a clear voice, 'Please stop saying that.' I always practise this with the child so that she can say it clearly and firmly. If children say it weakly it will not work. Also, if children say it angrily and loudly, it might provoke the bully.
2 Walk away — calmly, and without showing you are upset.
3 If neither of these works, tell the teacher.

A combination of problem solving and training in assertiveness can work well for children who are being teased or bullied. Typically, the children are seven to ten years old and have been picked on very cruelly and maliciously by others. This can go on for months, even years, and the children often become unhappy and moody. Usually I spend a lot of time using the problem-solving steps and getting the child to come up with a solution (or set of solutions) that she thinks will work best. Mostly the solutions include strategies of ignoring the bully or telling him firmly to 'Please stop.' We rehearse this until the child can do it well. If this does not work, telling the teacher is often an alternative. Of course the parents have usually suggested these things to the child many times. The difference is that in problem solving, it is the child who makes the suggestions.

> There are always exceptions to the usual solutions children come up with. Shane was nine years old. After spending some time using relaxation and getting him to calm himself down we went through the problem-solving steps. We came up with the usual ones of ignoring the bullying or telling the teacher, but Shane was convinced these would not work. When Shane was asked to evaluate which solutions would work, he thought there was only one — hitting the other boy. I discussed this with his parents and we sat down with Shane to point out the drawbacks — he might hurt the boy, he might get hurt himself, and it could escalate the situation. He would also get into trouble. Shane would not be moved.
>
> The next morning, when the other boy made a sarcastic remark to Shane, Shane hit him. Shane got into trouble at school, got a detention and was threatened with suspension. The other boy never teased him again.

Signs of being bullied regularly include:

- nightmares
- change in mood, and irritability
- stomach aches or headaches, especially the evening or morning before school
- not wanting to go to school
- not wanting to get on the school bus
- asking for extra food or money (to give to the bully).

If you notice these signs, talk to your child. Then you need to approach the school directly. All schools should have an anti-bullying policy and should treat this seriously. If this does not work seek help, such as a psychologist at your local community health centre.

I was seeing a nine-year-old boy, Michael, who was being teased every day by a group of boys. They greeted him in the morning by calling him names and followed him around at recess and lunch. Michael said he ignored them, but when I went through specific instances with him, it was obvious that he often answered back and sometimes got visibly upset.

We went through the problem-solving steps and I helped prompt the usual solutions, but Michael was not impressed and did not think they would work. Then he said, 'I know, I'll tell them a joke.'

He and his mother then spent the weekend searching for funny jokes. On Monday morning as he got off the bus, the three boys came up to him and started calling him names.

Michael said, 'Hey, do you want to hear a joke? Have you heard the one about ...?'

I would love to have seen the reaction of the boys.

At recess they came up to call him names again, but
Michael just had another joke to tell them. By the next day, they
gave up.

By telling jokes, Michael was not submitting or showing fear.
Nor was he giving them an emotional reaction, which they
wanted. It in fact showed that he was not afraid of them, so they
gave up.

You can help your children by talking to them about problems. When you ask about what they did at preschool or
school, do not let your child get away with, 'Nothing much.'
Ask what she did at recess or lunch, who she sat with, who
she played with and what they played. Occasionally ask if
anyone was mean to anyone else. Also ask if anyone was
mean to her. Don't ask this every day, just sometimes.

If your child tells you someone was being mean to her, use
this as an opportunity to help her problem solve.

In a nutshell

- Assertiveness can be used instead of aggression and instead of submissiveness.
- Model being assertive for your children.
- Being assertive means speaking in a clear, but not loud voice. This needs to be practised.
- Being assertive means looking directly at people when you speak to them.
- Being assertive means not being rude or angry.

Final comments

I wrote this book because of the crucial role that behaviour, social skills and problem-solving skills play in a child's development. This is not to deny the role of academic, language, artistic and physical skills, which are also important. However, if a child does not cooperate with parents or teachers, if he is rude to others and if he cannot deal with conflict, it is likely that he will not fulfil his potential. I have seen too many bright children who do not do as well as they should because of their attitude to learning. Helping your children do their best is what most parents want, and I hope this book helps you do that.

I have drawn on extensive research to describe parenting techniques that are effective. These are not just what I think; they are what the world's best researchers consider the most effective methods to use with children. I have also used these methods in my own clinical practice, so I have first-hand experience with how they work. These techniques are used by psychologists all over the world and are considered 'best practice'. My aim in this book is to make them widely accessible to all parents.

So do I use these techniques with my children? Not 100 percent of the time. I try, but like all parents, I get tired, I get cranky, I get irritable. There are times when I have lost my temper with them — and I still remember those times vividly. But most of the time I try to use the methods of raising children that I have described in this book. They do not always go perfectly according to plan, but I still think the methods are the best we can use.

If, as a parent, you work hard on Part 1 and concentrate on

improving cooperation and behaviour, you have given your child a great start. If you try the rest, it is an added bonus. How consistent do you have to be? It depends on the child. If you have a child who is verging on ADD, the more consistent you are the better. These children do not learn as quickly from rewards and discipline; consistency is the best approach. For other children, consistency is still important

And remember, you are human and will make mistakes. Do not berate yourself — just start again the next day.

The best thing we can do for our children is to invest lots of time and care in them in their early years. Gradually, as our children grow, they will become more independent. They will develop their own friendships, and their friends and teachers will have increasing influence. All we can hope is that we have instilled enough self-discipline, problem-solving skills and plain common sense to ensure that the path they take is a happy one. We can only do our best.

Appendix

Nature vs nurture — the science behind it

In Chapter 2 we looked at nature and nurture. In recent years there has been some fascinating research into how a child's brain develops. This research is starting to shed light on some interesting questions regarding how nature and nurture interact. For example:

- Why do four times as many boys as girls have behaviour problems or learning disabilities?
- Why are two-year-olds so terrible?
- When is the best time to teach children social and problem-solving skills?

The answers lie in the brain, the most fascinating wonder on the planet.

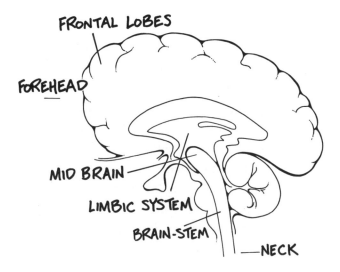

The brain and behaviour

The child's brain develops sequentially from bottom to top, starting with the base of the brain, just above the spine. This is called the brainstem. It is responsible for all those automatic functions that we do not think about — heart rate, body temperature, blood pressure etc. This part of the brain must be fully developed at birth, otherwise the baby will not survive.

The first 12 months

The next part of the brain to develop is just above the brainstem, and is called the midbrain. The midbrain is responsible for regulating sleep and appetite, and this is particularly important in the first 12 months. Until this is developed properly the child cannot get into a regular sleep cycle or start to develop mealtime habits.

The brain of the terrible twos

After this the limbic system develops. The limbic system is the centre for emotion. The reason we have a limbic system is that it is important for survival. For example, if you are just about to pick something up and you see a spider underneath it, you startle, pull your hand away, and feel a strong emotion of fear. All this happens without thinking. The limbic system is responsible for this rapid reflex and the upswell of emotion. The limbic system is there so that we feel fear as well as other emotions and get out of trouble quickly.

The limbic system starts to develop around 18 months, and becomes very active at this time. It is no coincidence that at this time our children become very good at showing emotions: screaming, crying, throwing tantrums, hitting or biting. This is the terrible twos.

The years three to seven

Between the ages of three and seven the frontal lobes develop more fully. The frontal lobes are just behind the forehead and are the 'thinking' part of the brain or, as psychologists call it, the area of 'executive function'. The frontal lobes are responsible for thinking, problem solving and planning. Importantly, connections between the frontal lobes and the limbic system also develop at this time. Through these connections the frontal lobes start to exert some control over our emotional limbic system.

Think of it as a telephone system, where the frontal lobes have just been connected to the emotional limbic system. The frontal lobes can now 'phone up' the limbic system and tell it to calm down. The connections act like a brake on the child's emotions.

Being the thinking part of the brain, the frontal lobes help the child start to think rationally about her emotions. So if another child snatches a toy, instead of hitting or crying, the child may now think, *Well, he's only little, he can't help it*, or *If I hit him, I'll get into trouble.* So she stops herself reacting, and her thoughts tell her not to get quite so upset.

This is also the age when there are dramatic increases in language. This helps children express their thoughts and feelings.

The connections between the frontal lobes and the limbic system are a vital part of a child's development. We know that these connections are heavily modified by the child's experiences. So if parents teach the child that tantrums do not work, and teach alternative appropriate behaviours, this develops strong connections between the frontal lobes and the limbic system. As these connections strengthen, the child gradually learns to control her emotions. The optimum time to teach the child this self-control is between the ages of three and seven, when these connections are forming. It is possible to do it later, but it takes more time and patience.

On the other hand, if the parent lets the child get her own way, or is inconsistent, these connections fail to develop. The limbic system will fire, but the frontal lobes have not been trained to modulate the emotional impulses. Interestingly, children with ADD have less frontal lobe activity than other children, and it is thought that this is why they are less able to control their impulses. Drugs such as Ritalin (methylpheni-date), which is used for ADD, act by stimulating the frontal lobes so they have more control over the limbic system. They reduce the impulsiveness of children with ADD in this way.

Girls and boys

Sugar and spice and all things nice, that's what girls are made of ...

In the preschool and primary years, it is boys who have more behavioural and emotional problems than girls (though girls catch up in adolescence). In fact, boys are more likely than girls to be diagnosed with ADD and/or ODD (Oppositional Defiant Disorder, and to have learning difficulties and language problems. Recent evidence points to one possible reason for this. Male and female embryos start life in the uterus with no differences (apart from chromosomes). Male and female embryos both have girl parts and boy parts to start with. In the sixth week of pregnancy, in males, the testes start to secrete testosterone. It is thought that in some males, the brain might be overly sensitive to the testosterone, or too much testosterone is secreted, causing damage to certain parts of the brain. It seems that this damage might be one factor causing speech and learning difficulties. Fortunately, all is not lost. While the brain is still developing it is remarkably resilient, and other parts of the brain can take over functions of the damaged parts.

Author's notes

Page 7 **Almost one in five children today has behavioural or emotional difficulties:** Zubric, S.R., Silburn, S.R., Garton, A., Burton, P., Daldy, R., Carlton, J., Shepherd, C., & Lawrence, D. *Western Australian Child Health Survey: Developing Health and Wellbeing in the Nineties,* Bureau of Statistics and the Institute of Child Health Research, Perth, Western Australia, 1995.

Page 7 **In recent years prescriptions to children for fluoxetine (Prozac) and sertraline (Zoloft) … have increased fivefold …:** Clavenna, A., Bonati, M., Rossi, E. & De Rosa, M., 'Increase in non-evidence based use of antidepressants in children is cause for concern', *British Medical Journal,* March 2004, vol. 328, p. 712.

Page 9 **18 percent of children continue to have significant behavioural or emotional difficulties:** Zubric, S.R., Silburn, S.R., Garton, A., Burton, P., Daldy, R., Carlton, J., Shepherd, C., & Lawrence, D. *Western Australian Child Health Survey: Developing Health and Wellbeing in the Nineties,* Bureau of Statistics and the Institute of Child Health Research, Perth, Western Australia, 1995.

Page 11 **There is growing evidence that children with good social skills …:** McClelland, Megan & Morrison, Frederick, 'Pre-school social skills more critical than academics', *Early Childhood Research Quarterly,* July 2003.

Page 13 **Some psychologists claim that emotional intelligence is more important than IQ:** Goleman, D., *Emotional Intelligence: Why it can matter more than IQ,* Bantam Books, New York, 1997.

Page 18 **Thom Hartmann gives an interesting theory about how ADD genes …:** Hartmann, Thom, *Attention Deficit Disorder: A Different Perception (A hunter in a farmer's world),* Underwood Books, Grass Valley CA, 1997.

Page 21 **Many of the Romanian refugees were adopted by caring Canadian families and Canadian researchers have followed their progress:** Lemare, Lucy, 'Tracking the progress of Romanian orphans', *Simon Fraser University News,* October 2003, vol. 28, no. 4. See also www.sfu.ca/mediapr/print/sfu_news/archives_2003/sfunews10160317.htm; www.adoption-research.org/chapter3.html.

Page 34 **Children get around four times more attention for negative behaviour …:** Reid, J.B., Patterson, G.R., & Snyder, J., *Antisocial Behaviour in Children and Adolescents,* American Psychological Association, Washington DC, 2002, p. 80.

Page 34 **Some ancient societies were very advanced in their thinking about play:** French, Valerie, 'History of Parenting: The Ancient Mediterranean World', in M.H. Bornstein (ed.), *Handbook of Parenting: Volume 2, Biology and Ecology of Parenting,* Lawrence Erlbaum Associates, Mahwah NJ, 1995, pp. 263–84.

Page 35 **A recent study …:** Coleman, Priscilla, 'Parent–child relationships aid social skills', Bowling Green State University, December 2003. See www.bgsu.edu/offices/pr/news/2003/news3361.html. See also Cohn, D., Patterson, C. & Christopoulos, C., 'The family and children's peer relations', *Journal of Social and Personal Relationships*, 1991, vol. 8, pp. 315–46.

Page 38 **A recent study in the UK …:** Cited in the *Sydney Morning Herald*, 5 August 2004.

Page 39 **Many children died in their teens, literally of overwork:** De Mause, L., 'The evolution of childhood', *The History of Childhood Quarterly*, 1974, 1, pp. 503–75. See also www.psychohistory.com/childhood/writech1.htm.

Page 45 **In one study in Atlanta, Georgia …:** Long, P. Forehand, R., Wierson, M., & Morgan, A., 'Moving into adulthood: Does parent training with young noncompliant children have long term effects?', *Behaviour Research & Therapy*, 1994, 32, pp. 101–107.

Page 48 **According to some authors …:** Porter, Louise, *Young Children's Behaviour: Practical Approaches for Caregivers and Teachers* (2nd ed), MacLennan & Petty, Sydney, 2003.

Page 49 **There is abundant evidence for this:** Slaby, R.G., Roedell, W.C., Arezzo, D. & Hendrix, K., *Early Violence Prevention: Tools for Teachers of Young Children*, National Association for the Education of Young Children, Washington DC, 1995, p. 64. See also Forehand, R. & Long, N., *Parenting the Strong-willed Child*, Contemporary Books, New York, 2002, p. 94.

Page 52 **… the words you say convey only about 7 percent of the meaning:** Pease, Alan, *Body Language: How to Read Others' Thoughts by Their Gestures*, Camel, Sydney, 1981.

Page 60 **In fact there has been a fair bit of research on nattering.** Patterson, G.R., *Coercive Family Process*, Castalia Publishing Company, Eugene OR, 1982, p. 69.

Page 67 **In ancient Rome, fathers had the right to take the life of a newborn as well as their other children:** French, Valerie, 'History of Parenting: The Ancient Mediterranean World', in M.H. Bornstein (ed.), *Handbook of Parenting: Volume 2, Biology and Ecology of Parenting*, Lawrence Erlbaum Associates, Mahwah NJ, 1995, pp. 263–84.

Page 90 **Research has identified five main skill areas …:** Hauser, R.M., Brown, B.V. & Prosser, W.R., *Indicators of Children's Well-Being*, Russell Sage Foundation, New York, 1997.

Page 95 **Studies show that children … whose parents play …:** Coleman, Priscilla, 'Parent–child relationships aid social skills', Bowling Green State University, December 2003. See www.bgsu.edu/offices/pr/news/2003/news3361.html.

Page 98 **Children who attend preschool or childcare are generally more socially competent than those who do not:** Clarke-Stewart, K.A., Allhusen, V.D. & Clements, D.C., 'Nonparental caregiving', in Bornstein, M.H. (ed.)

Handbook of Parenting, Vol. 3, Lawrence Erlbaum Associates, Mahwah NJ, 1995, p. 162.

Page 101 **Couples who take time to say hello and show some form of affection** ...: Gottman, J.M. & Notarius, C.I., 'Decade review: Observing marital interaction', *Journal of Marriage and the Family*, 2000, 62, pp. 927–47.

Page 107 **My colleagues and I recently published a study** ...: Cooper, J.A., Paske, K.A., Goodfellow, H. & Muhlheim, E., 'Social skills training to reduce aggressive and withdrawn behaviours in childcare centres', *Australian Journal of Early Childhood*, 2002, 27(4), pp. 29–35.

Page 108 **Some Californian psychologists** ...: Lovaas O.I., Schaeffer, B. & Simmons, J.Q., 'Building social behaviour in children by use of electric shock', *Journal of Experimental Research in Personality*, 1965, 1, pp. 99–109.

Page 108 **It is a fact of life in preschools that one-half of all attempts by children** ...: Webster-Stratton, Carolyn, *How to Promote Children's Social and Emotional Competence*, Paul Chapman Publishing (Sage Publications), London, 1999.

Page 114 **A survey found that 35 percent of teachers** ...: Walker, H.M., Ramsey, E. & Gresham, F.M., 'Heading off disruptive behaviour', *American Educator*, Winter 2003/2004, pp. 1–14.

Page 117 **Research shows that parents who talk to and read to their children** ...: Hart, B. & Risley, T.R., *Meaningful Differences in the Everyday Experiences of Young American Children*, Paul Brooks Publishing Company, Baltimore MD, 1995.

Page 117 **On the other hand, parents who are depressed** ...: Cox, A.D., Puckering, C., Pound, A. & Mills, M., 'The impact of maternal depression in young children', *Journal of Child Psychology & Psychiatry*, 1987, 28(6), pp. 917–28.

Page 133 **In the 1950s, researchers at the Johns Hopkins School of Medicine** ...: Williams, J.E., Patton, C.C. & Siegler, I.C., 'Anger proneness predicts coronary heart disease risk: prospective analysis from the artheroscelerosis risk in communities (ARIC) study', *Circulation*, 2000, pp. 2034–39.

Page 140 **Joe Simpson, in *Storms of Silence*** ...: Simpson, J. *Storms of Silence*, Mountaineering Books, Seattle WA, 2000.

Page 141 **Daniel Goleman, author of *Emotional Intelligence*** ...: Goleman, D., *Emotional Intelligence: Why it can matter more than IQ*, Bantam Books, New York, 1997, p. 199.

Page 147 **Anxiety affects one in ten children:** Rapee, R., Spence, S.H., Cobham, V. & Wignall, A., *Helping Your Anxious Child: A Step-by-step Guide for Parents*, New Harbinger Publications, Oakland CA, 2000.

Page 147 **Children who have been abused are in a state of alert all the time:** Moore, Mary Sue, 'Patterns of attachment in infants and children', lecture presented at Prince of Wales Hospital, 3 May 1991.

Page 180   **... 80 percent of all aggressive acts between young children ...:**
Reid, J.B., Patterson, G.R., & Snyder, J., *Antisocial Behaviour in Children and Adolescents*, American Psychological Association, Washington DC, 2002, p. 80.

Page 180   **Research indicates that aggressive children are more likely to pick on children they can make cry ...:** Patterson, G.R., *Coercive Family Process*, Castalia Publishing Company, Eugene OR, 1982, p. 69.

Page 180   **In one study, mothers told their daughters to give up something ...:** Preuschoff, G., *Raising Girls*, Finch Publishing, Sydney, 2004.

Page 185   **Studies show that squabbles ...:** Schroeder, C.S. & Gordon, B.N., *Assessment and Treatment of Childhood Problems: A Clinician's Guide*, Guilford Press, New York, 2002.

Page 185   **Frank Sulloway argues that sibling rivalry is 'in the genes' ...:** Sullaway, F.J., *Born to Rebel: Birth Order, Family Dynamics, and Creative Lives*, Pantheon Books, New York, 1996.

Page 197   **Recent evidence points to one possible reason for this:** Hill, J. & Maughan, B., *Conduct Disorders in Child and Adolescence*, Cambridge University Press, Cambridge, 2001.

Further reading

Arthur website: www.pbskids.org/arthur.

Brett, Doris, *Annie Stories.*, Hale & Iremonger, Sydney, 1989.

CASEL (Collaborative for Academic, Social and Emotional Learning) website: www.casel.org.

Centre for Effective Parenting website (excellent resource for parenting information — click on parent handouts): www.parenting-ed.org.

Cooper, J.A., Pearson, L., Goodfellow, H., Paske, K. & Mulheim, E., PALS (Playing And Learning to Socialise) Social Skills Program, Inscript Publishing, <www.palsprogram.com.au>.

Forehand, R. & Long. N., *Parenting the Strong-Willed Child*, Contemporary Books, New York, 2002.

Garth, Maureen, *Moonbeam: A Book of Meditations for Children*, HarperCollins Publishers, Australia, 1992.

Manassis, Katharina, *Keys to Parenting Your Anxious Child*, Barron's Educational Series, New York, 1996.

Offerman, L. & Moroney, T., *Happy Face, Sad Face: A First Book About Feelings*, Five Mile Press, Melbourne, 1999.

Oram, H. & Joos, F., *All-Better Bears*, Anderson Press, London, 1999.

Preuschoff, G., *Raising Girls*, Finch Publishing, Sydney, 2004.

Rapee, Ronald M., Spence, Susan H., Cobham, Vanessa and Wignall, Ann, *Helping Your Anxious Child: A step-by-step guide for parents*, Oakland CA: New Harbinger Publications, 2000.

Stimson, J. & Lewis, J., *Worried Arthur*, Ladybird, Loughborough UK, 1994.

Watanabe, S. & Ohtomo, Y., *Hello! How Are You?*, Bodley Head, London, 1979.

Acknowledgements

I would like to thank my wife, Helen, for her wonderful support in writing this book. Thanks also to my two children, Nicola and Martin, for their love, help and understanding in a very busy year and for providing me with funny stories.

I am indebted to all the families I have worked with over the years for teaching me what books can not.

I would like to thank Rex Finch, my publisher, who gave me this opportunity and also my editors, Sean Doyle, Sarah Shrubb and Kathryn Lamberton for their encouragement, patience and hard work.

Thanks to Natalie Traynor for her feedback and encouragement regarding the early drafts.

John Cooper

Other Finch titles of interest

Understanding the Woman in Your Life
A man's guide to a happy relationship
Steve Vinay Gunther
This entertaining, no-nonsense guide
is full of relationship-saving advice,
delivered with warmth as well as the
occasional wake-up punch.
ISBN 1876451 67X

Parenting for Character
Equipping your child for life
Andrew Mullins
A practical guide to assist parents in
encouraging their children to think
independently, to develop habits that
lead to good character, and to make
choices that are good for themselves and
others. ISBN 1876451 661

Your Child's Emotional Needs
What they are and how to meet them
Dr Vicky Flory
This unique book explains the
connections between children's emotions
and their behaviour, overall wellbeing,
friendships, school performance and
their ability to adjust to adolescence.
Ages 0–12. ISBN 1876451 653

Raising Girls
*Why girls are different – and how to help
them grow up happy and strong*
Gisela Preuschoff's advice ranges from
birth to late adolescence – and across
physical and sexual development,
schools and learning, gender
stereotyping, parent–child relationships
and the daughter's emotional life. ISBN
1876451 599

Adolescence
A guide for parents
Michael Carr-Gregg and Erin Shale
In this informative and wide-ranging
book, the authors help parents
understand what is happening for young
people aged 10–20 and how to deal with
it. They discuss the big questions in a
young person's life and provide parents

and teachers with useful approaches for
handling problems. ISBN 1876451 351

Teen Stages
How to guide the journey to adulthood
Ken & Elizabeth Mellor
One of the Mellors' key concepts
is that teenagers grow through six
developmental stages, each requiring
specific responses that rarely work for
the others. To help parents and teachers,
the Mellors offer numerous practical,
tested suggestions about what to do and
how to head off 'trouble' before it starts.
ISBN 1876451 386

Lessons from my Child
*Parents' experiences of life with a
disabled child*
Cindy Dowling, Neil Nicoll & Bernadette
Thomas
The stories in this book have been
contributed by parents of children with
intellectual and physical disabilities.
What emerge are rare and honest insights
into the reality of raising a disabled
child and a powerful reaffirmation of the
strength of love. ISBN 1876451 548

Starting School
How to help your child be prepared
Sue Berne
How a child starts off at school plays
an important role in determining their
approach to education throughout life.
This book will help you ensure that your
child's practical, emotional and social
skills are sufficiently developed to make
the most of starting school.
ISBN 1876451 475

A Handbook for Happy Families
*A practical and fun-filled guide to
managing children's behaviour*
Dr John Irvine
In this wise and humorous approach
to parenting, the author tackles the
commonest problems with children of all
ages. He also presents his innovative and

well-tested 'Happy/sad face discipline system', which draws families together rather than dividing them.
ISBN 1876451 416

Raising Boys

Why boys are different – and how to help them become happy and well-balanced men (2nd edition)
In his international bestseller, Steve Biddulph examines the crucial ways that boys differ from girls. He looks at boys' development from birth to manhood and discusses the warm, strong parenting and guidance boys need. ISBN 1876451 505

Raising Boys Audio

A double-cassette set read by Steve Biddulph. ISBN 1876451 254

Confident Parenting

How to set limits, be considerate and stay in charge
Dr William Doherty
This book shows you how to parent effectively and how to ensure that your family is not overwhelmed by external pressures such as advertising, TV, and peer culture. ISBN 1876451 467

Fathering from the Fast Lane

Practical ideas for busy dads
Dr Bruce Robinson
The pressures of working life today mean that many fathers are not spending the time with their children that they would like. In this collection of valuable fathering ideas, over 75 men from various backgrounds speak about ways to improve this situation and how they balance demanding jobs with being a good dad. ISBN 1876451 211

Parenting after Separation

Making the most of family changes
Jill Burrett
So much parenting now takes place from two households, following separation. This book offers positive approaches to helping children and making the most of these family changes. ISBN 1876451 378

Stepfamily Life

Why it is different – and how to make it work
In Margaret Newman's experience, stepfamily life is different, and therefore different solutions are needed to get it 'on track' – and, more importantly, to help it survive. Margaret considers a wide range of stepfamily scenarios, and gives practical suggestions as to what to do in each case to overcome any difficulties.
ISBN 1876451 521

Father and Child Reunion

How to bring the dads we need to the children we love
Dr Warren Farrell
This book calls for a rejoining of families (and of children with parents who can care for them) by creating equal opportunities for men as parents.
ISBN 1876451 327

Bullybusting

How to help children deal with teasing and bullying
Evelyn Field reveals the 'six secrets of bullybusting', which contain important life skills for any young person. Activities introduce young readers to new skills in communicating feelings, responding to stressful situations and building a support network. An empowering book for parents and their children (5–16 years). ISBN 1876451 041

On Their Own

Boys growing up underfathered
Rex McCann
For a young man, growing up without an involved father in his life can leave a powerful sense of loss. On Their Own considers the needs of young men as they mature, the passage from boyhood to manhood, and the roles of fathers and mothers. ISBN 1876451 084

Chasing Ideas

The fun of freeing your child's imagination
Christine Durham teaches thinking skills to children, and in this book she

encourages parents and teachers to see how discussing ideas with their children (aged 4–14) can be an enjoyable and creative activity for everyone. ISBN 1876451 181

Fear-free Children

Dr Janet Hall draws on real-life case studies to help parents overcome specific fears and anxieties that their children have, such as fear of the dark, fear of being alone or fear of animals. ISBN 1876451 238

Fight-free Families

Dr Janet Hall provides solutions to conflicts in a wide range of family ages and situations, from young children through to adolescents. ISBN 1876451 22X

ParentCraft

A practical guide to raising children well (2nd edition)
Ken and Elizabeth Mellor's comprehensive guide to parenting provides clear information on issues such as communicating with children, a healthy (no-hitting) approach to discipline, the stages of child development and skills in managing families. ISBN 1876451 19X

Men after Separation

Surviving and growing when your relationship ends
Ian Macdonald
'Men often react disastrously to a marriage ending. This book gives a frank and direct approach to men's practical concerns, emotional needs, sexuality, and the importance of clear and rational thinking. Highly recommended (*Steve Biddulph*). ISBN 1876451 610

The Happiness Handbook

Strategies for a happy life
Dr Timothy Sharp
'Happiness is no more than a few simple disciplines practised every day; while misery is simply a few errors in judgement repeated every day.' So says Dr Sharp, founder of the Happiness

Institute in Australia and author of *The Good Sleep Guide*. ISBN 1876451 645

Emotional Fitness

Facing yourself, facing the world
Cynthia Morton's innovative program of 30 'emotional workouts' helps individuals learn how to overcome difficult issues in their lives, care for themselves and ultimately reach self-acceptance. These workouts have been successfully used in sessions with individuals and groups. ISBN 1876451 580

Bouncing Back

How to overcome setbacks, become resilient and create a happier life
Brian Babington outlines some approaches to cope with the initial trauma of loss and failure and to find ways to recover. His approaches help people who have experienced severe loss – such as a death in the family – or other traumatic events, such as the breakdown of a relationship or the loss of a job. ISBN 1876451 564

Sex-life Solutions

How to solve everyday sexual problems
Respected sex therapist Dr Janet Hall offers clear and practical step-by-step directions for solving all types of sexual difficulties. The book includes sections for men, women, and couples, as well as one on anxieties based on mixed messages and misunderstandings about sex. ISBN 1876451 408

Take Control of Your Life

The five-step plan to health and happiness (2nd edition)
Dr Gail Ratcliffe
This book is a blueprint for recognising what is wrong with your life, minimising your stress and maximising the opportunities to reach your goals. The author, a clinical psychologist, has developed her five-step method of life-planning and stress management with clients for over 13 years. ISBN 1876451 513

Manhood
An action plan for changing men's lives
(3rd edition)
Steve Biddulph tackles the key areas of a
man's life – parenting, love and sexuality,
finding meaning in work, and making
real friends. He presents new pathways
to healing the past and forming true
partnerships with women, as well as
honouring our own inner needs.
ISBN 1876451 203

Dealing with Anger
Self-help solutions for men
Frank Donovan
Focusing on emotional healing and
practical change, this book includes
case studies from clients of the author
(a psychotherapist) and a program of
exercises for the reader. ISBN 1876451 05X

The Body Snatchers
How the media shapes women
Cyndi Tebbel
From childhood, women are told they
can never be too thin or too young. The
author exposes the rampant conditioning
of women and girls by those pushing
starvation imagery, and encourages us to
challenge society's preoccupation with
an ideal body that is unnatural and (for
most) unattainable. ISBN 1876451 076

A Strong Marriage
*Staying connected in a world that pulls
us apart*
Dr William Doherty believes that
today's divorce epidemic is the result of
overwhelming and conflicting demands
on our time, rampant consumerism, and
the often skewed emphasis we place on
personal fulfilment. This book shows
how to restore a marriage worth saving
– even when it seems too late.
ISBN 1876451 459

The Partner Test
How well are the two of you suited?
This entertaining and informative
book gives couples insights into their
relationship. Twenty tests cover
important issues associated with

attraction, compatibility, commitment,
life together, intimacy and sex,
communication and expectations.
ISBN 1876451 602

Side by Side
*How to think differently about your
relationship*
Jo Lamble and Sue Morris provide
helpful strategies to overcome the
pressures that lead to break-ups, as well
as valuable advice on communication,
problem-solving and understanding
the stages in new and established
relationships. ISBN 1876451 092

Boys in Schools
*Addressing the real issues – behaviour,
values and relationships*
Edited by Rollo Browne and Richard
Fletcher
Positive accounts of how classroom
teachers have implemented innovative
approaches to help boys' learning and
their understanding of relationships.
ISBN 0646239 589

Kids Food Health
Nutrition and your child's development
The authors, Dr Patricia McVeagh – a
paediatrician – and Eve Reed – a dietitian
– present the parents of children from
newborns to teenagers with the latest
information on the impact of diet on
health, growth, allergies, behaviour and
physical development.
Kids Food Health 1: *The first year*
ISBN 1876451 149
Kids Food Health 2: *From toddler to
preschooler* ISBN 1876451 157
Kids Food Health 3: *From school-age to
teenage* ISBN 1876451 165

*For further information on these and all
of our titles, visit our website*: www.finch.
com.au

Index